Oh B

Oh Boy!

Mothers Tell the Truth About Raising Teen Sons

MARYANN BUCKNUM BRINLEY

THREE RIVERS PRESS • NEW YORK

Published by Three Rivers Press, New York, New York.
Member of the Crown Publishing Group, a division of Random House, Inc.
www.crownpublishing.com

Three Rivers Press and the Tugboat design are registered trademarks of Random House, Inc.

Printed in the United States of America

Design by Helene Berinsky

Library of Congress Cataloging-in-Publication Data
Brinley, Maryann Bucknum.
Oh boy! : mothers tell the truth about raising teen sons / Maryann Bucknum Brinley.—1st ed.
p. cm.
1. Mothers and sons. 2. Teenage boys. I. Title.
HQ775 .B67 2004
649'.132—dc22
2003015706

ISBN: 1-4000-4526-6

10 9 8 7 6 5 4 3 2 1

First Edition

This book is dedicated to
the Saint Kitts Rum Company,
makers of Brinley Gold . . .
a family adventure that makes me
smile almost as much as
Bob, Zach, and Maggie Brinley.

Contents

ACKNOWLEDGMENTS   13

INTRODUCTION   15

The Art of Being Smart   23
STAY AWAKE FOR NIGHT GAMES

The Art of Not Panicking   28
UNDERSTAND HIS EMERGING SEX DRIVE

The Art of Climate Control   36
CHOOSE CALM OVER CLEAN

The Art of Staying Sane   42
EXPECT SIGNS OF MATURITY AT UNEXPECTED TIMES

The Art of Ego Building   48
SHOW HIM SOLUTIONS

The Art of Real Experience   55
STOP WORRYING

The Art of Reading Signals   61
PICK UP ON OBSCENE PHONE CALLS

The Art of Making Mistakes   69
CHECK YOUR ASSUMPTIONS

The Art of Being His Secret Weapon   74
RECOGNIZE HIS ARMOR

The Art of Manipulation
SHARE THE PAST

79

The Art of Practicality
BE READY FOR BEER BONGS

83

The Art of Listening
STAY CLOSE

88

The Art of Crying
DON'T HIDE RAW FEELINGS

94

The Art of Getting Rid of Guilt
PLAY HIS GAME

103

The Art of Learning the Truth
SEEK SECRET ALLIES

111

The Art of Opening Closed Doors
GIVE IN

120

The Art of Being Brave
OPEN YOUR MIND

127

The Art of Blaming Genes
LIKE FATHER, LIKE SON

135

The Art of Stopping Resentment
RECOGNIZE TOXIC EMOTIONS

142

The Art of Communication
HEAR WHAT HE'S NOT SAYING

150

The Art of Cursing
MATCH CODE FOR CODE

156

The Art of Loving Like a Rock
GO ALONG WITH PUPPY LOVE

161

The Art of Hanging In There
RIDE ALONGSIDE HIS TURMOIL

167

The Art of Biting Your Tongue
SEARCH FOR SIGNS OF INTELLIGENT LIFE

173

The Art of Being Content 177
ACCEPT HIM

The Art of Rescue 183
GO TO SCHOOL

The Art of Making the Last Move 189
FOLLOW YOUR INSTINCTS

The Art of Exercising Good Judgment 196
TRY DISCIPLINE

The Art of Winning 204
SNIFF OUT THE RATS

The Art of Imperfection 212
PERFECTLY SAFE IS IMPOSSIBLE

The Ultimate Art of Unconditional Love 216
DIG DEEP AND THINK OF YOURSELF AS AN
ARTIST OF HUMAN NATURE

Acknowledgments

For their creative contributions, I would like to thank Darrick, Kitty, John, Doris, Bud, Marc, Cindy, Kevin, Joyce, Tyeshom, Liina, Eileen, Ben, Linda, Wes, Gay, Travis, Marsha, Jeremy, Gemma, Arlene, Howard, George, Sandy, Sassan, Janice, Matt, Sheila, Len, Marco, Maureen, Tom, Trina, Danny, Ana, Carlos, Tom, Oneida, Justin, Dede, Pete, Dennis, Rick, Mary Ann, Mark, Andrew, Susan, Zach, Tamara, Caleb, Penny, David, Gail, Carmel, Noah, Leslie, Saidou, Andrea, Troy, Anita, Brent, Diane, Brian, Patty, Adam, Geoffrey, Brenda, Ari, Robin, Di, Terrence, Gary, Sara, Sid, Saul, June, Kevin, Timmy, Lorraine, Anne, Billy, Kathy, Jason, Julie, Armand, Carolyn, Wes, Arlene, Vinnie, Carmen, Christopher, Bernice, Irene, Bilal, Noah, Lois, Jake, Elizabeth, Ian, Harb, Andria, Lamar, Katie, Kavish, Cyndi, John, Adam, Mike, Scott, Billy, Difie, Wade, and many others with whom I've shared teen boy stories in the last four years.

On the home front, if it weren't for Bob, Zach, and Maggie, I would have given up on this project long ago. A special thanks is due for letting me read aloud on the journey to the finish line.

Introduction

I was outside the Budget Print Center on the corner of Cooper Avenue and Valley Road in Upper Montclair, New Jersey, when I stopped to reconnect with a friend.

"Oh boy," she says. "Wait until you hear what's going on."

Her son is fourteen years old, six feet one, 180 pounds, a sturdy, big boy and on the freshman football team. She picked up the thread of a story from school about some boy who peed into an empty beer bottle and then offered it to a ninth-grade girl at a party. (Yes, word is that the girl drank it, which could certainly make a body very sick.) This mom is worried about her son's inability to think clearly. He's made some pretty screwy choices in the past. Was he the boy who gave the girl the tainted beer bottle?

" 'Aw Mom,' was all he could say in defense at first," she laments. "His tone of voice just reeked with denial, but you never know. I had to push him and dig hard to get the truth."

Here in her life are the real secrets of parenting boys through the amazing and turbulent teens. There are no formulas. There is no standard practice. Each son and each mother is an individual, and what happens between them is art, by even the most dictionary-like definition available: "Human effort to imitate, supplement, alter, or counteract the work of nature [a boy]." Or, on the other hand: "A specific skill in adept performance, conceived as requiring the exercise of intuitive faculties [by a mom] that cannot be learned solely by study." We may not always like the process or the outcome. It may not be pretty at all. But, oh boy, is that mothering. Ah yes . . . and every mother knows so.

At the ice hockey rink in the early morning cold or after a freezing late-night game, my conversations with other mothers of teen boys are priceless. "Listen. Listen," my conscience demands. Here are important insights from artful mothers who have been badgered too often of late. These secrets are not sanitized. These boys are not depressed or destined for prison. These mothers are artists. Their stories are gratifying—especially if you are also the mother of a teenage boy. "So . . . you've been there too," they say.

When I e-mail friends who are struggling with murky mothering issues regarding boys thirteen through eighteen and even nineteen, I see what it feels like to mother a pubescent child of the opposite sex. "He nearly killed his younger brother. He put his hand through the wall in his bedroom. His father doesn't want to deal with this issue."

In empathy, when I dial the number of a mother whose son is currently the butt of a soccer team joke and afraid to go to school as a result, I try to reach for intimate wisdom, not the kind delivered dispassionately by someone with letters that follow a last name. "Did this ever happen to Zach?" she asks. Zach is my own son, who is now twenty-four. "Well, sure . . . sort of . . . I know how you feel. High school hallways can be emotional minefields."

Sharing stories and secrets with women who are right there with us doing the psychological and physical "dirty" work of raising teenage boys reinforces a truth I learned working with Kay Willis of Mothers Matter in Rutherford, New Jersey. "Following an expert's advice," says Kay, "doesn't make you an expert, it just makes you a follower." In other words, real experience, expertise, and the art of mothering can be found in the lives of real women. This is what I am trying to capture in *Oh Boy*.

We parents of adolescents have heard a lot from Harvard psychologists, from fathers, and from boys themselves, as well as from legions of university-trained scholars. I've read the best-sellers and wise books about boys, from *Raising Cain* by Dan Kindlon, Ph.D., and Michael Thompson, Ph.D., to Olga Silverstein and Beth Rashbaum, authors of *The Courage to Raise Good Men*. All these books are beneficial, of course, but isn't there more to be shared from women themselves? How to take your male child through the turbulent adolescent years and arrive together safe, sane, and secure on the other side of twenty-one has been such a hot topic. Sometimes the advice is wonderful and deeply reassuring. We need it. Sometimes the wordy discussions never even enter the realm of reality for the mothers I've met. As one friend insists, "I'm tired of experts telling me what I'm doing wrong. I just want a book to keep nearby so I can see that other mothers are experiencing the same ups and downs."

I wrote this book because mothers of adolescent boys need to know that they are unsung heroines. In order to reap any insight from this book, you ought to:

Stop feeling guilty.

Expect to find reassurance or a few laughs.

Pat yourself on the back and say, "Aw Mom," you *are* doing a good enough job.

Take some time off for your own good behavior. Being the mother of a teenage boy seven days a week, twenty-four hours a day can tip the balance of your sanity scale. To be on top of his game, you need to be in good shape mentally.

All stories are pulled from real life, hundreds of interviews, and encounters I've had with mothers all across the country. I'd like to think that the incidents are universal and that they cross cultural and geographical lines, and I have purposely avoided using pseudonyms for my moms and sons. Instead, I simply refer to them as "she" and "he."

In order to protect these good and sometimes new friends, as well as their remarkable sons, from further exposure or ridicule down the road, identities and anecdotes have been merged and altered. These topics are delicate and I would never want to be the catalyst for a confrontation between mother and child. At a time in life when privacy can become an integral part of growth, let's face it, "You told her *what?*" could easily turn into a battle cry.

Yet I'd be a cad if I didn't show some recognition in print for all the honesty I heard in my research in Montclair, New Jersey; State College, Pennsylvania; Wallace, North Carolina; Boise, Idaho; Edinburg, Texas; Kirkwood, Missouri; Atlanta, Georgia; Sanibel Island, Florida; Vashon, Washington; San Diego, California; El Paso, Texas; Shreveport, Louisiana; Norfolk, Virginia; Fort Madison, Iowa; Livingston, New Jersey; Villa Park, Illinois; Hubbard, Iowa; Brooklyn, New York; Laurel, Maryland; Calama, Washington; Indianapolis, Indiana; Albuquerque, New Mexico; Boston, Massachusetts; Quechee, Vermont.

I begin each anecdote with a brief introduction to the "art" of mothering. In these sections are tips, voices, quotes, and even a few old news clippings I've collected along the way to my own son becoming twenty-five this year. You need all the help you can get as a mother and, for me, that means picking up signs of my superiority when I see them in print or in some researcher's evidence. You may feel some of these ideas are quirky. Skip over them when that happens. Some are serious.

Feel free to jump around in this book. And forgive me if any-thing I say comes off as expertise. I am no expert. I've just spent years interviewing the people who like to call themselves experts.

Each introduction should lead you into the nitty-gritty encounters and the earthy truths that emerge when you are on the front lines of life with big boys. They are big boys with lit-tle boys' brains, and isn't it true that as grown women we sometimes wonder how far we should go, what we should do, whom we should call? You may not find any encounter that matches your own experience as a mom. Sorry about that. I also decided to steer clear of really heartbreaking or life-threatening incidents. I did find a few stories of suicide, acci-dental death, and serious mental illness, but my light-touch format in this book couldn't do those mothers' tales justice.

What you will find are little dramas told by mothers of ado-lescent boys. Honestly, don't we really want to know what other mothers think and what they are doing? There's nothing more reassuring to a mom in the middle of a crisis than know-ing that other women have been there and lived to tell the tale. During pregnancy, we were offered detailed descriptions of every single stage and step. Our babies', toddlers', and young children's lives were carefully mapped in millions of ways by experts from all walks of life as well as other mothers. Yet, regarding adolescent boys, the significance of our power is heard almost only in whispers or between the lines written by doctors and dads. William Pollack, author of *Real Boys: Rescu-ing Our Sons from the Myths of Boyhood,* puts so much control in our court that he believes "the time has come to encourage women to trust their instincts when it comes to mothering a boy." Even Daniel Kindlon, author of the hugely popular and wonderful *Raising Cain: Protecting the Emotional Life of Boys,* credits the close connection to his mother as "perhaps most valuable of all" in his own success. He writes that it is a mother's love and guidance, especially during adolescence, that provide "the emotional education" a boy needs to flourish. In "the connection" with his mother, the man should always be able to "find the place where he is loved best of all." If you don't call this a tall order to fill, I don't know what is. Yet, the art of making this right "connection" is exactly what overworked, underappreciated moms are asked to cough up under pressure all the time.

My hope is that *Oh Boy!* will help you do just that.

Oh Boy!

The Art of Being Smart

A team of researchers at the University of Richmond in Virginia led by psychology professor Craig Kinsley has discovered that motherhood can make us smarter and may even help prevent dementia. Honestly, I love these kinds of studies. They were working with rats, not real women, but the results were still amazing and reassuring to those of us who have thought that our IQs would drop on account of the mothering maze.

At the annual meeting of the Society of Neuroscience in Orlando, Florida, in the fall of 2002, Kinsley announced, "When people think about pregnancy, they think about what happens to infants and the mother from the neck down. They do not realize that hormones are washing the brain. If you look at female animals who have never gone through pregnancy, they act differently towards young. But if she goes through pregnancy, she will sacrifice her life for her infant—that is a tremendous change in her behavior that is manifested in genetic alterations in the brain. Females who had two reproductive experiences were able to learn and remember the maze better than females with one or zero." This research team believes that the effect may be even more pronounced in humans, because we invest significantly more time in raising our young than rat mothers.

Now watch how this mother flexes her intelligence quotient.

Stay Awake for Night Games

So, she wonders why he is being so nice to her this evening. He's been grounded for more than a week and has been, until this moment, surly even beyond what she can believe, and she certainly knows this kid's every emotional lurch. Sigh. He can really hurt her and usually succeeds. You know his type. Maybe you have one at home. Handsome, tall for sixteen, and uninterested in academic success, he's the quarterback on the high school football team, though only a junior. That doesn't mean she still can't exert control, which, of course, she's been doing since the guidance officer pointed out his unexcused absences and his report card with nothing but C's and that B in Italian, which everyone knows is a gimme from the assistant football coach. It hasn't been easy since his dad died when he was in middle school. But she's surviving nicely, and his two older brothers—one still in college and the other already out in the working world—are proof of her single-mother moxie.

Now, tonight, a Saturday, this youngest son has decided to go to bed at 10 P.M.

"I'm really beat, Mom," he says sweetly.

She's not really buying this recent helping of sugared talk

but it does feel nice. "Okay, I'm going to finish watching my movie but I'll be up soon."

"Good night," he hollers, taking two steps at a time.

Now she hears him thump down the upstairs hallway and into the bathroom. There's the sound of water running and he crosses over to his bedroom. Maybe he really is sleepy. You wish . . . but not a chance. He did have football practice in the morning and then spent the entire afternoon working for the lawn service moving shrubs for the Clarks, who are putting in a new front walk. Anyone else would be exhausted but—and here's that tiny nagging truth of unconscious knowledge coming to the surface—she knows that this son could never be tired on a Saturday night at ten. A world of possibilities would keep him awake no matter what. The social life he was missing right now must be playing a riotous tune inside his head. She just knows it. There had been numerous calls to his cell phone. Not once did he return those messages within earshot of her.

She doesn't pause the movie but decides to let it play on. In fact, she turns the volume up loud. He thinks she is losing her hearing anyway, so let him become convinced. Sliding into her pink slippers and buttoning her sweater, she gets out of the Naugahyde recliner and quietly tiptoes across the family room to the attached screened porch. She looks around. The light from the kitchen window sheds only a little clarity on the lawn. Is there anything amiss? She can't tell and to tell the truth, she doesn't really know what she is looking for.

Outside, the air is miraculously crisp and very breathable. It had been warm and humid earlier in the week, especially for such a late fall time of year. So sticky. But now it's gorgeous outside. A night to remember. She crosses the backyard to the garage but doesn't want to flip on the light. What if he is watching her from his bedroom window? This has to be a surprise, she knows . . . and then wonders, what is it that should come as a surprise? This reminds her of that song in *West Side*

Story, the one in which Tony and Maria both sense that "something's coming, I don't know what it is, but it is . . . gonna be great." Forget it. Focus, she tells herself. What is he up to?

His bike? Hey, the bicycle is missing. Grabbing a flashlight from the shelf on the garage wall, she heads back around to the side of the house. His room is at the rear corner with windows facing back as well as to the side. Bushes and overgrown shrubs make passage painful but she pushes through. In the pale yellow beam of the light in her hand, she spots it: the waiting bike.

But she can wait, too.

The sound of the movie still playing inside the TV room is clear. Those windows are open and the voices travel easily in the still night air. Is he going to wait until the movie has ended? She hopes not because that will be another hour at least. Lately he's been locking his bedroom door anyway, so he can't fear being exposed to a potential good-night kiss from her. No, the bigger fear would be missing out on any action to be grabbed from this Saturday night. She guesses that he'll make his break while the television noise can still act as a buffer. And she's right.

Now sitting in a lawn chair to the side of those bushes, with an unobstructed view of both of his bedroom windows, she hears the sound of his bedroom screen window being clicked out. From inside, a rope comes tumbling out. He is using a piece of old clothesline, and she can't believe he would be this stupid. He might get hurt. Don't shout, she tells herself. Hold it. Don't move yet.

He looks out, checking to see where his rope has dropped, and throws one leg over, then the other. Waiting for just the right time to expose his folly, she sits tight, completely still. He is so strong and so handsome and so young. Wow, what his father wouldn't have given to see him now. Stop that, she says. Don't go there. He's easing himself down the clothesline. What's it attached to upstairs? she wonders.

He lands on the back porch roof with a thud. Thank goodness, he didn't have to go the full two stories to the ground. She thinks, Wouldn't that line have caused rope burns? Maybe all the landscape and yard work he's been doing has toughened up his palms, not to mention all that palming of the football night and day.

As he scurries over to the end of the roof and prepares to jump down, she shines her light directly on him. What a look of absolute shock. I win, she thinks. I win.

"MOM? What the hell are you doing there?" he screams.

"A better question, I think, is what the hell are you doing there?" she replies but not in a scream. A sweet pleasurable sensation comes over her. There haven't been very many occasions lately when she has won this game they play.

"Well, you know. . . ." He is fumbling, dropping his ballsiness.

"I guess I do know," she says. "Want to put your bike back in the garage now or in the morning?"

It's still gorgeous outside. And yes, this is a night to remember, she tells herself as she tries not to smile. Now is not the time to laugh. Yet, her ability to outsmart him is fun for her to consider. As she heads back into the house, he jumps off the porch roof. He's going to move the bike out of the bushes tonight. She starts wondering what she'll do when he heads off to college in two more years. Her job is certainly not challenging. If she really is so smart, maybe she'll go back to school and finish the course work for the degree she was supposed to get before he was born. That's a good idea.

The Art of Not Panicking

Signs of puberty start when he's only nine or ten. Your son is still a child, and my guess is that no adult tells him much at first. His testicles and scrotum (areas of his anatomy that you may not have seen in some time), once close to his body, drop at about age thirteen. Nipples swell on some boys. This is called gynecomastia and it's temporary. If you were he, would you share these facts of life with you? Michael Riera, dean of students at Marin Academy in San Rafael, California, and author of *Uncommon Sense for Parents with Teenagers*, says that your son may not know as much as you think he does, even in this no-holding-back world of media sex and Internet adventuring. "In an ideal world, the road to sex" (and the drive starts with hormonally whipped-up, developing boy and girl bodies) "is paved with lots of information and conversation about its mechanical and emotional aspects."

The truth is, we moms feel a bit out of our element in this arena. And with ignorance can come a bit of panic. Schools aren't very helpful either, according to *Time* magazine. "The standard curriculum now consists of one or two days in fifth grade health class dealing with anatomy, reproduction and AIDS prevention, and perhaps a twelfth grade elective course on current issues in sexuality." Even so, when we stumble into wisdom, sometimes we discover just how much we do know. Here is a mom who turned her shock around in time to say exactly the right thing to her son.

Understand His Emerging Sex Drive

He's seventeen and still a virgin. That's a comfort to her but not to him. You will recognize her, I'm sure. Though we mothers aren't all alike, certainly not, our minds just don't head naturally, instinctively into the same places as our sons'. Meanwhile, she knows the part about his virginity because he wrote an essay anonymously complaining that every other guy in his high school class had crossed this mighty river of passage. Of course, what he doesn't know, but she does, is that boys will lie about such things.

But he is still so young, a really young seventeen, not even ready to jump from her comfortable nest in their midwestern town. Nothing to worry about. This will take time. The separation issues and the sex are elements of mothering she takes in stride, most of the time. He can't see anything clearly right now. She didn't mean to read the essay. It was right there on the computer when she went on-line. Called himself El Virgino. Ouch.

"Maybe I haven't found the right girl," he has typed. Of

course he hasn't, she thinks. His hair is dyed Kool-Aid pale green. He uses tubes and tubes of L'Oréal Ironing Gel every morning to make it stand out and up. Oh my, he may be seventeen, which in some cultures makes a man mature, but not here, not now. He's a child. Still her child. "If I stay with a girl long enough, I might be able to reap the sexual reward," he admits. "Reward?!!!" She cringes for him and for herself when he rattles on, jealously describing in his teenage prose how most of his friends are studs.

Recently he has been upstairs on the computer all the time. Working on that paper for American history, he says. Researching colleges, he explains. In the ritual eleventh-grade spring one-on-one, his guidance counselor gave them a list of possibilities, including a few famous "reach" schools. He is taking those practice SATs so the next set of scores will go up, she hopes. She's sent off the check on time for another round of standardized test-taking and his admission ticket has arrived in the mail. He's definitely been distracted lately. His grades aren't as good as they were last year, either. He's also in the chat rooms, she knows, having shut her out of some places in his mind. He doesn't talk to her as much and she theorizes that it's good that he's communicating with friends, after all. Yet, he's up there tapping away so late into the night, and he's so removed from the rest of the family. What do they talk about? That is, if you can classify on-line chat and e-mail as human contact and communication. She's the kind of mother who never bought into the idea of a TV in every room—no set for every child's television taste—preferring to have her brood around her even when it meant bickering about choice of sitcoms and professional wrestling shows. After all, chaos, even that family fighting kind, connects them intimately. The disconnections are what worry her more.

It's three o'clock on a Thursday afternoon and she's just

come in the back door from school. Her seventeen-year-old puzzle is at the gym, pumping iron with pals. His little brother is at soccer practice. Her husband won't be home until at least six or maybe a little later tonight because he had a meeting in Indianapolis.

"Hey Mom, do you remember that e-mail address for your old friend at the agency in New York?" her eldest daughter asks. "I'm thinking of sending her my résumé."

"Oh sure," she says. "If I don't have it on my Rolodex, I know it's somewhere in the old address book on the computer."

An hour later, when the honeyed turkey breast is in the oven, the small red potatoes are scrubbed and ready to go, the salad is set, and the dishwasher is emptied, she climbs the stairs to what had been more of a full-time office back when she was freelancing five days a week. Now it's considered family turf and not just her own space. She flips on the computer, waits for the beeps and whirs of the hard drive connections to stop, and begins to search for that old computer address file for her daughter. It's not in the main directory. Remnants of her seventeen-year-old are all around. Why, she wonders, can't he put anything away, ever? Piles of paper clutter the desk. An empty, grossly congealed glass of what must have been one of his nutritional, calorie-boosting shakes sits alongside the keyboard. Energy bar wrappers are on the floor to the left of the wastebasket. Did he narrowly miss or purposely trash the office floor? Hmmm. Absently ticking off a mental reminder to bring his trash habits up later at dinner, she clicks her way into the windowed maze of a world he seems to prefer to her these days.

What is it about the Internet that is seductive to some seventeen-year-olds? she wonders. Pulling down a history menu, then aiming for a default drive, up pops a highway of stunning sites. Suddenly, anxiously, with heart beating wildly, she reads:

FREE PORN . . . Angelfire . . . Melissa (Is that a friend of his? Maybe) . . . *Amateur Teen Babes . . . Peefantasy* (Ohhhh, shhh-hhhhh . . . oooooot. She doesn't say *shit*, though it's her favorite expletive. She's been working to change that habit.) . . . *Tempted Teens . . . Space Amazones . . . Call Girls—The Celebrity Hardcore . . . BabylonX—Palace of Pussy! . . . Teens 18–21 Sex Erotic Pictures . . . Extremely Hardcore Wrestling . . . New Mega Porn Site! . . . Increase Your Ejaculation by 30% . . . Increase Your Sexual Potency by 75% . . . V-Force with Peruvian Maca Root to Enhance Sexual Performance . . .* (maca root? Oh wow.) Sweaty palms. Stomach sinking.

No? Couldn't be? Not her son? Could be! So this is where he's been going. She clicks onto Angelfire, hoping to find angels with wings or stories about firefighters, and instantly, the most amazingly, graphically accurate, anatomical image of a woman's vagina covers the entire screen. In fact, for a second, she doesn't even realize she is looking at a vagina. There's no face to be found. Thump. Thump. Thump. That's her own heart thumping. Angelfire—could that be a real name?—has intimate parts that don't appear to be those of a human because they are so enlarged and intensely in focus.

Whew. She sits in the desk chair she bought earlier in the summer at Staples on sale. Good buy. (Our minds are capable of latching on to the strangest bits of cognitive string for survival at times. She actually thought of the bargain-buy chair right then.) What to do next? What to do at all? Frozen to her seat, she takes a deep breath. Yes, breathe deeply. In through the nose. Out through the mouth. That's right. Just as the calm-voiced yoga instructor croons. In her seat, she thinks about how everyone in her family had been complaining about using the old rocking chair whenever they worked on the computer. She had broken down and bought a real executive office chair that swivels and fits the curve of the lower back, but it's not comfortable at all right now. Should she call his dad? Where exactly would he be? In the car? Still at his meeting? Swiveling around to face the door behind her, she wonders about that Peefantasy site. Someone out there has linked pee to fantasy to create a single word. Now that makes her really uncomfortable and icky all over. Is he sick? Is this normal?

Footsteps on the stairs. Stop. Breathe deeply. You can do this. You'll survive.

"Hey Mom, did you find the address yet?"

Oh no. Her daughter can't help but see the image of Angelfire's private parts framed behind her on the computer monitor.

Eyes wide, mouth open, her twenty-two-year-old registers the vagina image and shrieks, "MOM! What are you doing?"

"Oh no. No. No. I didn't. I mean it's not me," she says, swiveling back around to click away and erase the tracks of her son's on-line sexual adventures. "I didn't. I mean it's your brother. I didn't go there. He did."

"Awwwww, he is so sick," his sister says.

Really? Sick? Later, still sitting upstairs at the computer, waiting for him to arrive home from the gym so she can confront him with the printed directory list of his virtual escapades, she can't help but be furious with him as well as the perverts who put up these sites. How dare they prey on inexperienced teenagers with raging hormones and infinite sexual curiosity! Oh, but Peefantasy?!! A computer's history tells the truth so clearly, even down to the time allotted each encounter. . . . Did that really say fourteen minutes in Peefantasy?

It dawns on her that she knows where his concentration wasn't going—toward that SAT scheduled for Saturday morning. And she can see lots of reasons why her scared seventeen-year-old might want to escape that test-taking burden. (I wouldn't want to have to brave SATs again, would you?) In fact, why would a boy click onto the SAT practice site if he could go to Angelfire instead?

She sits there awhile, wondering, calming herself, playing with options. Her daughter has gone downstairs to finish up dinner preparations. Half an hour later, this mom is still in her Staples chair when she can hear him coming upstairs. His sister has sent him straight up, per her orders. Head low, he comes around the corner and looks in at her before slumping into the rocking chair, as far away from his mother as he can get while still being in the same small office. She thinks, oh my, that's the same chair she used to rock all of her babies to sleep in. This one, this child in front of her, had such a hard time letting go at night . . . never sleeping soundly through until nearly a year after his birthday. Is he sleeping soundly now? Bet not.

"Are you okay?" she asks. Not so angry anymore. Just curious now. Yes, she's really curious about the sticky web he's woven for himself. "Are you all right?" she repeats.

"I don't think so, Mom." He's scared, she can see that—but not of her. "I think there's something really wrong with me."

She says, "I think you'll be fine."

Getting up from her nearly new swivel office chair, she moves toward him, and he doesn't flinch when she leans down to put her arms around him. He lets her hold him awkwardly. She adds, "Lots of men have been right where you are and they turn out just fine."

The green is growing out. All that gel is now sweat-sticky but he'll be okay. She knows he'll be okay because what he's dealing with is a very natural, basic, human sex drive. Yet, isn't it amazing, she thinks, what havoc this urge can create inside a fearful adolescent boy? She also thinks that the next best step is to sit down with his dad so these two guys in her life can take an intellectual walk through some of these untouchable topics, man-to-man.

"Aw Mom, do you really think I'm okay?" he asks.

"Sure you are. This is perfectly normal, but let's get your dad in on it."

"Okay."

By not panicking in this particular encounter, this mom has regained her son's trust. And that feels so nice, even though she will have to go into the computer's hard drive to erase all the pornographic cookies on her system. She's not happy about that at all.

The Art of Climate Control

The mess in some of our boys' rooms can create storms of angst. Of course, you can close the door on the upheaval. That's certainly a good idea if the garbage and clutter are going to interfere with your unconditional love for him. It's the only way to go for some of us. Pull the door. Shut it tight. You can't do it all. You shouldn't even try. Let him grow up or find himself in need of something lost in the madhouse. Admit it: You can choose to nag and get angry when faced with a carpet that has grown moldy beneath a wet towel, or in the frantic search for a missing worksheet describing the parameters of a science project worth 20 percent of a grade (and probably crumpled into a ball under his bed). You can also sneak into his space and clean it yourself. I'd do that and Zach, my son, was pretty easygoing about my intrusions into his privacy. All boys aren't so copacetic about this kind of interference, however.

Cleanliness isn't next to godliness. But I think it might be right next to the gene for maturity, and maybe some of us simply aren't born with this in our genetic makeup. One of my very best friends is on the messy end of the clean-to-clutter spectrum. That doesn't make her less than beautiful and intelligent. She is both. Other things are more important. I had another wonderfully wise friend who devoted her life to making sure mothers realized that the atmosphere at home—not the interior decorating or level of cleanliness—was the single most important factor contributing to a child's ultimate happiness and success. Let this be your gift: climate control. She used to say, "Forget about good housekeeping and decorating. What's the climate like in your home? Is it stormy? Would you want to live there? Are you comfortable? Cozy?"

There is a saying that you can never go home again, but I disagree. You can. You do it all the time. Isn't it true that you take the memory of your home wherever you go?

What's more, every once in a while, some outside force that we never expected comes to our rescue. In this story, a letter from a customer service center was just what this mother and son needed to clean up and grow.

. . . .

Choose Calm over Clean

He is thirteen. She hasn't been able to get anywhere near the corners of his bedroom for as long as she can remember because of the piled-high clothes, sports equipment, toys, trash, baseball cards, last year's science projects, and who knows what else. These, however, are his treasures. "Please don't touch." Okay by her. His domain belongs to him. She doesn't really mind, except on school mornings when treasure hunts for homework assignments or lost items make them both crazy. When she does clean through in a quick sweep, she sticks to the worn paths, picks up the obvious, and has decided this is just not something she can afford to fixate upon. Though at times, on warm, muggy days, that overall emanating odor on passing his doorway isn't very appealing, there are too many other more pressing matters in her life.

She is fresh from a divorce that was years in the making. In more than twenty years of marriage, she was pregnant four times and gave birth to five children. Yes, there were twins. Life hasn't been so sweet for some time. The climate of control disappeared long ago. Oh yes. Storms of anger even sent her husband packing. Yet, this child just on the threshold of emotional puberty and emerging from a year of hormonal upheaval is kind of fun to have around. You just have to overlook the mess he trails behind. A younger version of herself would have been unable to see past his faults, but she's almost cool. No big deal. He feeds her mother hunger in so many other ways. Besides, she notices that other boys his age are drooping, sagging, bedraggled, and uncombed, too.

"Sign of the times," she says to me as I pass her on my way to the post office one sunny afternoon in June and pause to talk about his unkempt look. I'm kind of pleased to see her smile because she is so thin—stressfully, not purposefully. She's been battered emotionally. For some of us, eating when angry or in turmoil is not a given. Others of us only dream of shaving a few inches off thunder thighs.

"How is he doing?" I continue. I know he's on her worry list for social and academic reasons. Also, sometimes it's easier to talk about our kids than it is to head straight into ourselves.

"He's good, really good. This has been a good year at school, in fact," she answers. "Do you know where he is right now?"

"No, where?"

"He's upstairs there," she says pointing to the second-floor window. "Cleaning his room. I didn't even ask him to do it. This is on his own."

"Whooaaa. What happened?"

"His PlayStation," she explains. "He is in love with this PlayStation he got for Christmas. We still had the box so when it burned out, we packed it up and sent it back to Sony's customer service center. They repaired and returned it but he also got a letter yesterday explaining why it died."

"Why?"

"Dust!" she says. "It was overcome by dust and dirt."

We both start laughing.

"Never in my wildest dreams would I have been able to come up with such a motivator for him to clean up his room. Mr. Clean, I love it. You should have seen the look on his face when he read the letter from the service department."

In a stormy frenzy upstairs, he is rediscovering pieces of his past. This is a slow-going process, not something he wants to rush through, even though he'd rather be outside, where the climate today is nearly perfect. A box of big black trash bags sits on the floor and sorted piles have taken shape. There is no one else who can do this for him. He knows that. He doesn't want her help. She might make a mistake and trash something really valuable. She doesn't always see stuff the way he does. Holding up a battered baseball cap, he knows she might not understand. He'd never throw this one away. It's a keeper. And there under his bed is his baby blanket. He doesn't want to take it into bed with him anymore . . . at least not all the time. Frayed and missing the blanket binding, which had been his favorite part, the blanket could easily be mistaken for a rag.

Here's the secret: It smells like his mother. She's a keeper, too. Now he spies some old Game Boy cartridges. They can go. He's got his PlayStation back and intends to keep it operational.

"How are you coming with your cleaning?" she asks from his bedroom doorway.

"Fine. Fine. I don't need any help."

"Of course you don't," she says. "I'm just going to put some things here by the door . . . things you might need." She's dragged the vacuum, a dust brush, pan, rags, and a mop to the doorway. "I can show you how to use these if you want."

"Nah." He shrugs.

"Really, I promise not to get into your stuff."

"This cleaning is hard," he admits.

"Yeah, especially the part you're at right now. It's really hard to let go, isn't it? To throw out stuff."

"I don't want to, Mom."

"I know you don't."

"But I want my PlayStation to stay clean," he says.

"Keep at it," she says. "You'll feel so good later. Growing up is hard. I never wanted to either."

When she steps out of his sight, he reaches under the bed for that old blanket, a remnant from a time in both their lives when they weren't buffeted by bad weather. This stormy state is nearly over. A birthday next month and high school in the fall will cool everything down. In fact, his life is about to turn a corner, and she is so happy that he is emerging from this postdivorce state with a clear head. The fact that he is cleaning on his own is a little treasure for her today.

Down in the kitchen, she gets a little teary with the knowledge that the clean room is just a small part of this day's dilemma. Her life needs to change just as much as his will in high school. Take this house, for instance. It reminds her too much of her ex-husband and the happy times way back when.

Like her boy, she needs to clean out sad reminders of the recent past and move on. The real estate market is still hot in her town, but who knows how long that will last in a badgered economy. Calm now, she stops crying, and before she can talk herself out of it, she dials the phone number of the real estate agent across the street, the friend who has been urging her to make a clean sweep of her life.

The Art of Staying Sane

....

Every now and then, in fact more or less at yearly intervals during the teenage years, nature puts on the brakes and effects a sudden and sharp turn in a young person's behavior," say researchers Louise Bates Ames, Ph.D., Frances L. Ilg, M.D., and Sidney M. Baker, M.D. The mother who related this next story to me wasn't always able to see or focus closely on where her son was going because of everything else swirling around in her life. Mothering a son single-handedly is one thing, of course, but just how would years of legitimate anxiety about life and death affect a boy? Someone once said that the line between sanity and insanity is narrow and we all walk on either side from time to time. This mom certainly has every reason to have spent more time on the insane side than the rest of us. Her husband's failing kidneys, his need to stay tethered to regular dialysis appointments, and all three of them waiting for him to reach the top of the organ donor list kept the entire family on a lethal razor's edge for years.

But she's strong and staying sane, nevertheless. Even Sigmund Freud, who didn't recognize the power of a mother over her child for most of his working life, would have to agree. Freud always emphasized father love, as clinical psychologist Robert Karen says in *Becoming Attached: First Relationships and How They Shape Our Capacity to Love.* "Just before his death, Freud spoke with some feeling about the power of the tie to mother, describing it as 'unique, without parallel, laid down unalterably for a whole lifetime, as the first and strongest love-object and as the proto-type of all later love relations—for both sexes.'"

Here a mother wrestles with issues from the past as well as her son's future.

Expect Signs of Maturity at Unexpected Times

She wakes up at 4 A.M. to knocks on her bedroom door. A single mom for more than two years now, she has just welcomed her eighteen-year-old son back from the University of Florida, where he had tried a freshman year away from their Queens, New York, home. Let's just say that he was not ready to be away from home. He needed her, she needed him, and one semester was enough to let them both know the truth. He didn't fail any of his courses. She thinks that too much turmoil had churned them both up emotionally as well as physically. So, he'll be starting his spring classes in the city. Wants to be a musician. Perfect for him. A career path that may drive her crazy, but she doesn't say that out loud. "Boys are like aliens, certainly from another planet, and sometimes you do want to kill them, but they can also be very sweet." She chuckles.

Just last year, this boy with the shaggy long hair, clear dark eyes, and serious musical talent had been diagnosed with a condition that required ten hours of back surgery. This came not long after her husband's death from botched kidney transplant surgery.

But this is about a 4 A . wake-up call, I think. Not these deep, burrowing background issues.

"He had gone to sleep early," she says.

"Oh really?" I answer. My expression must show a bit of disbelief.

"Really. No, seriously, I know he was tired and we've been through so much together that this isn't the kind of kid who needs to play games with me about his whereabouts or his intentions."

She remembers a time when her husband was alive when he told his father that he just didn't understand girls.

"Why?" his dad asked.

"Well, this girl, a friend of mine, asked me if she looked fat in a skirt." (God, isn't that classic of us to ask the men in our lives these useless questions?)

So his dad said, "Did you know what to say?"

"Well, obviously not, because she isn't speaking to me anymore."

"What did you say?"

"I told her she didn't look fat in that skirt, which of course she interpreted as her looking fat in other skirts."

She loves her son immensely and patience has been her mantra. But not at 4 A.M. There have been too many sleepless nights, and she has only just begun to dream deeply again, after years of anxiety about her husband's failing kidneys, the twice-weekly dramas of dialysis, the donor waiting lists, and then the end, suddenly and too soon. Let's not even mention money worries. Don't wake her up. This woman has earned her rest.

But the knocking continues. Then the door to her bedroom opens.

"Is that you?" she asks.

"Yeah, it's me. I didn't want to worry you."

"You're waking me up," she announces.

"Well, I thought you might be worried about me," he says.

"I'm asleep," she says. "Or I was asleep. And you were asleep. So why would I be worried?" The garishly illuminated dial on her bedside clock glares 4:14 now.

"Well, I thought you might have gotten up to go to the bathroom and noticed that I wasn't in my bed and then gotten scared," he tries to explain. " 'Cause when you went to sleep, I was already asleep."

"Where were you?" she asks angrily.

"Ma, just wait a minute, cool it," he says. "Megan beeped me because she was afraid to be alone. Her parents are out of town this weekend and she heard a noise in her apartment."

"You went over to Megan's in the middle of the night?" she asks.

"Well, yeah. She was really scared. I checked everything out to make sure she was safe." Megan is a friend who lives several blocks away in their Queens neighborhood. While the streets are fairly safe in their area, nothing is ever absolutely without danger in New York City at 3 A.M. out in the dark.

"How long did you stay?" she asks.

"Until she fell asleep. Then I walked back home."

"What if you had found somebody in her apartment?" She sits up, even more wide awake with fear than minutes before, as the possibility of a disaster creeps into her consciousness. "With a gun? Or a knife?"

"Oh Ma. I'd know what to do," he reassures her.

"You would?" she asks.

"Sure," he says, and kisses her good night. "Go back to

sleep. I'm sorry I woke you but I just wanted you to know that I was home safe."

She doesn't go back to sleep immediately but lies there thinking about that line between sanity and insanity and how her son has managed to stay on the safe side.

"There were so many things going on here in his life when he was growing up that I am amazed at his staying power. He can be so direct, so calm, even when confronted with the worst situation. How did that happen? I remember, when he was twelve and had to do a report on an illness for health class, he chose kidney disease. Can you believe that? Oh sure, we had always been straight with him about his dad's condition, but well, this was so raw. He videotaped his father for this class project," she says.

On the tape, with no script, he asks his father point-blank about the disorder that will one day kill him.

"How ya doin', Dad?"

His father answers, "Well, not so well. I've got very serious kidney disease."

She stops her recollections, possibly picturing the rest of this weighty father-and-son face-off on the old film. Those were the worst of times, of course, but now she can see them also as the best of times.

"You know," she continues, "he had a really bad period of time after his father's death and one day he went into his bedroom for a couple of hours. I knew he was having a hard time but I also knew he had to go through this on his own, at least part of the way. When he came out later, he said to me, 'Ma, tomorrow you can be depressed. Okay?'

" 'Sure.'

" 'We'll take turns.'

"That's what we did," she recalls. "We took turns being depressed. I tried not to break down when he did. That's how we got through his father's death."

An alien? From another planet? I don't think so. He's on the safe side of that line between sanity and insanity, maturity and childhood, because of her own very powerful gravitational pull.

She is so proud of him that she's even willing to forgive being awakened at 4 A.M.

"I have to go look for that tape he made of his dad," she says, realizing that she may be able to watch it now without breaking down emotionally. She tried once, unsuccessfully, right after the funeral. Remarkably, even in the face of his own death, her husband had stayed artfully sane, and she knew that his son—her son—would be able to do so as well.

The Art of Ego Building

O ur impression of ourselves is the single most telling factor in determining our ultimate success or happiness," says psychologist Wayne Dyer, Ph.D. During adolescence, dramatic physical changes can send all kids into rocky personal terrain, and boys are definitely not exempt from the body image wars. One of the things that I learned along the way through my son's adolescence is that in this art of ego building, a little empathy may go a long way. Sit still for a second and put yourself in his place.

Your boy may have strange, fluffy little outcroppings of facial hair about now. Pimples and zits, not only on his poor face but perhaps on his chest, shoulders, and back, have appeared. His hair turns greasy almost immediately after a shower. Sweat is no longer little-boy-sweet but really stinky and he's still trying to wear his favorite shirt every day. The BO can really catch you off guard and you don't know how to break it to him. The other morning when you went in to wake him for school, his penis was visibly standing straight up, possibly six inches, beneath his sheet. Are you wondering if he knows how to masturbate? Is that something boys understand without instructions from someone?

Yes, moms are in a foreign land without a translator or a map sometimes. Guess what? So is he. And, as one friend once reassured me, helping teenagers to believe in themselves is a show-and-tell exercise. You've got to be there for them to believe in themselves. The mom in this little story used her parenting instincts to nudge her son toward a healthier ego.

Show Him Solutions

"So he wouldn't let me sign him up for soccer camp at Penn State," she tells me. "He had really enjoyed it the summer before and I was kind of surprised by his refusal. He was adamant. I couldn't budge him, and yet, almost all the other kids on his freshman team were going to attend the same session and live in the dorms together. Even the junior varsity coach, for whom he'd be playing in the fall, had recommended that the kids go to camp together." She is frustrated with her son. He is fifteen and very unhappy with his body.

"When the coach called, I couldn't explain why he wouldn't go," she admits, remembering her embarrassment. An excuse about a family wedding saved the situation, but she was uncomfortable and concerned about him. Still little-boy skinny and in tenth grade, he anguishes about how tall he will be someday and whines about when he is going to grow. There is just so much pressure on teens today to look a certain way. Eating disorders are epidemic. The girl next door had to be hospitalized for anorexia nervosa. Deep down, she suspects that he backed out of camp because he was afraid of the teasing he might have to endure from the other, bigger boys on his team. Why do size and shape have to matter so much? We can't all look like supermodels or superstar athletes. Just try telling that to a son who is tormented by his size or shape.

Some mornings, she catches her son standing in front of his closet mirror flexing his biceps. Closing his fist, pulling the arm slowly toward his bent chin, he watches himself and waits for those little "guns" to emerge. That's what he calls his pip-squeaky muscles: guns. She can't help but smile.

"Oh honey, you are going to start growing soon. I promise you, it will happen," she says.

"How do you know?" Then he looks at her and asks, "Why can't you be taller?" Oh, so there is the blame now. His height is her fault. Maybe it is, in fact.

"We're just late bloomers," she argues.

Hardly anyone on either side of the family is tall. She is five feet two. His father is just five feet six, so the possibility of his remaining short is real. The tall genes just aren't there in this DNA mix. There are a few men on her side of the family tree taller than five feet ten. Maybe he will follow in their footsteps. Who knows? Don't remind him of that now. This boy is just under five feet and his build is slight. However, last year when he had to have an X ray because of a bad hip contusion, the orthopedist reading the X ray pointed out potential growth areas in the hip joints.

"I didn't start growing until my senior year in high school," says the doctor, who is at least five feet nine. That was nice. That hope the doctor held out is something her son depends on. She knows he's thought about it. Her reminders make him balk.

"Hey, just remember what the doctor said last year," she says too often.

"Yeah. Yeah. But when? When will I grow?" Yes, it has been a year since this pronouncement. So she wonders if there really might be something physically wrong with her son. Maybe she should ask the same doctor whether this boy is a candidate for growth hormones. But they can have side effects, she's read.

Other boys are taking supplements and bulking up by gulping nutritional shakes. It's no big deal, he insists. He wants to take creatine, a supplement that will supposedly "enhance" his workouts. Get that: He even uses the word *enhance* with his mother. There's that power of advertising. If everyone else is doing it, why can't he? Because she says no. What we don't know about supplements is enough to kill someone, that's why.

In my conversation with her, she tells me, "I'm totally against all this body-building culture. My god, all these little kids are lifting weights, working out, pumping iron, and I've heard that some coaches are encouraging the supplements. Is this right?"

In the fall, her son does go out for the soccer team again. She was afraid he might quit, but he hung in there. That makes her happy but, watching from the sidelines, she can see that his heart isn't in the game anymore. He's got to feel overshadowed by the big guys all around him. Even from across the field in the bleachers, she has no problem picking him out immediately. He is the shortest kid there. And he's not playing as much as he did in ninth grade. Soccer has been his love since first grade and he is a great little kicker. Her husband, who has coached town teams for years and is known as a harsh critic, says this boy has talent. Of course, her son thinks he can only be really great at this game if and when he gets bigger. When he does get onto the field during junior varsity games, he does fine. His corner kick is amazingly accurate. But the coach is not putting him in as much as last year. She wonders if his size is the reason or if his lack of confidence is showing. Of course, the lack of size is creating the lack of confidence, isn't it?

Late-blooming boys are in for a rough ride, aren't they? Can she do anything to help? Does she have to stand by lamely and watch him suffer? What a powerless feeling. She's beginning to think she should transfer him to a small private academy where the other students might be less inclined to tease. She tortures herself daily about keeping him in their town's big public school, with its diverse student body and high-pressure sports. His grades are fine. His sister loved it. And paying tuition for a private academy would cut into their college fund. They can't afford it. And she doesn't want to teach him to run away from his problems. Maybe he'll just take this battered ego with him in any move. But if she doesn't rescue him emotionally soon, maybe he won't even want to go to college. This is killing her.

Today there's a football game on the television in their family room. It's Saturday afternoon. Penn State is playing Michigan. The field goal kicker for Penn State is on the screen now, talking to coach Joe Paterno. This kicker is really skinny, and not very tall either. Obviously, there is a conversation about whether or not the field goal should be attempted. It's a go for the kicker. Paterno nods and sends him out onto the field. The ball goes through the uprights, and the fans go crazy. The kicker is ecstatic and so are his huge teammates. Say something. Do it now. This is your chance. Make him see a connection. Show him solutions to the inner dramas he's been building. He needs confidence more than a few more pounds and inches. She goes for it.

"Look at that kicker." Her son is about to use his command of the remote to cruise to another game, but he stops.

"What about him?"

"He looks a lot like you," she says.

No answer. He puts the clicker down now. She's trying not to hit him any harder with this link to his own life. Go softly, she thinks. Lead him to this idea of field goal kicking, but let him own it. This is his lifeline and he has to pick it up.

This Penn State kicker succeeds in making two more forty-five-yard goals that afternoon. Paterno, who rarely smiles, is shaking his head in pleasure.

"Pretty neat game?" she says, searching her son for a little feedback. What is he thinking?

"That guy used to play soccer," he says. The announcer had mentioned it.

"I thought so. He's not very big."

Silence.

"Seriously," she says. "You are such a good kicker."

Silence. Never the kind of kid who would easily acknowledge compliments, he's heard her, and the Penn State kicker has left the impression she wanted. Later that afternoon, her son grabs a football, not a soccer ball, and heads out to the field behind their house. From the kitchen window, she can see him practice for at least an hour. He's happy out there and he hasn't been happy in quite some time.

While one afternoon of field goal kicking is not going to solve all his self-esteem problems, she feels so good about this little corner he has turned. The truth is his ultimate success is going to be built on his own impression of himself, not how tall he grows or what others think.

Hey, she also wants to pat herself on the back for her leap of logic in linking her son's body drama to a skinny field goal kicker on television. Even if her own son never kicks a football after today, she doesn't care. His smile out there on the field is already having an effect on his brain chemistry. Maybe the surge in positive endorphins in his head will even start his growth spurt. Oh, but who cares about that? Not her. At least not today.

The Art of Real Experience

When your son is making you cringe with worry, for whatever reason, it's hard to focus on the plain truth that most boys are able to find themselves and get through the teen years without full-blown, scary identity crises. Keep this in mind to keep your fears at bay: Saying no really can come naturally during these adolescent years, and boys do need boundaries. But knowing when to say yes is also an important part of parenting. In fact, real experience is a better teacher than any restraints you put on him.

He's supposed to be trying on different identities. You can't always choose these roles for him either. Your son relies on peers, clans, clubs, music, culture, school, politics, and girls while he asks himself: Who am I? What do I want in life? He may also use falling in love as a pathway to young adulthood. As psychoanalyst Erik Erikson points out, "To a considerable extent, adolescent love is an attempt to arrive at a definition of one's identity by projecting one's diffuse self-image on another and by seeing it thus reflected and gradually clarified. This is why so much of young love is conversation." And, of course, it's also about making out, hooking up, getting it on, doing the wild thing, or whatever they call it in your neighborhood. Sometimes this can happen right on your front porch, as this story demonstrates.

We may want to hold him back, protect him from pain, or limit the reach of his life—especially when it comes to early sexual encounters—but that's not always possible or such a good idea anyway. The mother here was so happy she didn't take a stand about her son's choice of girlfriends but simply let nature take its course instead.

Stop Worrying

He is fifteen. Sometime in February, he arrives home from play practice with good news.

"Don't get your hopes up, Mom, but one of the prettiest girls in the junior class likes me. I think Kate, you know, Kate Mellonbach, is going to ask me to take her to the junior prom in May."

Her hopes? *Whose* hopes? Immediately she's wondering where in this unfolding drama she stands. Obviously, however, she's still standing squarely beside him in his mind's eye if his wishful thinking is so entwined with hers. She loves it. She hates it. She wonders what kind of mother-in-law she might be. Then she remembers that she absolutely adores her own mother-in-law. Here before her is a boy who has yet to have a single official "date," though dating is not exactly something his generation seems to do. He and his friends (which include some girls) hang out together, hook up, and go in groups, but as far as she can see, dates are few and somewhat foreign to the average fifteen-year-old. The junior prom would certainly classify as a date, but a date with an older woman? Oh wow.

Did she think *older woman?* Not nice. Not nice at all. This pretty, dark-haired, friendly, affectionate girl now waiting in the wings of his life is hardly older than he is in linear years. However, most of us realize, even if our pediatricians never point it out, that boys are about two years behind girls in physical and, no doubt, in emotional development. He is the younger guy. This basic image of her baby, coupled with the fact that this particular girl looks like, excuse me, a babe from *Baywatch,* stuns her. Kate even has her driver's license. Hmmm. Her mind races. Surprise should not be her knee-jerk emotion at all. After all, this is also the little boy with the collection of *Sports Illustrated* swimsuit issues under his bed and several raunchier magazines shoved to the bottom of his file desk drawer. (Honestly, she ran into both pieces of hormonal evidence by accident.) Perhaps if he had been following in older male siblings' footsteps, her own path would have been easier to see, but at this point, she is operating blindly. (Aren't we all?) Take a deep breath. Listen to him. Look at him. Don't jump to conclusions. Don't make a fool of yourself.

"Oh, how great," she answers. "How do you know this girl is going to ask you?" Ouch. Did she really refer to Kate as "this girl"? Did she strike that derogatory tone?

Now, word has come down through a loosely linked grapevine of friends who know friends who know Kate. She needs a date. She wants it to be him, her son, her fifteen-year-old with the braces and baseball cap on backward. Did he comb his hair today? Probably not. Yet he can hardly wait for the moment when Kate pops the question.

Finally, it happens. He is enthralled. Soon they are "going together" as well as going to the prom. February, March, April . . . the big night isn't until May.

She is perplexed . . . sort of. Please picture this. On a warm April evening, she and her husband hover anxiously in their upstairs bedroom, wondering if there is some parental protocol they are missing. They don't dare go to bed. Her son and Kate are making prom plans, and they have spent the end of a Saturday night with them watching television in the family room. How nice. Kate actually enjoys spending time at their house. She doesn't know what to do, how to behave sometimes. For instance, *Saturday Night Live* has long been over, and she knows that Kate's curfew has come and gone. She wonders which one of them—her son or Kate—took the precautionary measure of turning off the porch light. The two lovebirds have been kissing good night for a good twenty minutes, right there in the dark on the front-porch glider, a squeaky family heirloom. For once she's happy that no one has bothered to oil the rusty metal hinges. A partially open bedroom window just above is letting in more than fresh air tonight. The glider plays a chorus of night music she can almost translate in the squeaks, moans, and whispers—but not quite.

"What do you think they are doing?" she asks.

"Are you kidding?" Her husband laughs. "He's a teenage boy."

She sighs. The image of her son unhooking a D-cup bra would seem absolutely too hard for this mother to imagine, and yet, that's where she's going mentally. The only time in her life when she reached D personally was when she was breastfeeding the boy who's now on the glider.

"I'll give them five more minutes before I go back downstairs, make lots of noise, and flip on the porch light," her husband says. Good plan. She likes it. "That ought to break them up. Stop worrying," he reassures her. "She's a nice girl."

"I think that's why I'm worrying," she explains. "On the phone yesterday with Kate's mother, I couldn't help but get the impression that they were looking at our son as a long-term investment," she says. "The six of us—Kate and her parents, and the three of us—are scheduling a dinner together."

"You're kidding. He's only fifteen."

"Kate's parents met when they were freshmen in high school," she adds now to the uneasy mix. "Her mom thinks the kids make a great couple." Groan.

Our sons' first titillating sexual encounters certainly unnerve us. We want to know everything and, then again, nothing. This is all supposed to happen smoothly, naturally, stage by stage, step by step—but please, not now. Yet the absence of any male hormonal urges would make us just as crazy, I think. Where's the easy balance? That dream of falling in love with the perfect girl and living happily ever after is probably on every mother's wish list for her son, but does it have to come true midway through adolescence?

"Do you like her?" her boy asks later.

"She's really a great girl," she says, reaching for an enthusiastic range somewhere. Who wants to come across as an over-controlling, hard-to-please mother? Not her.

"Her parents are kind of crazy," he says.

Ah. He's been thinking and watching closely, she can see. The behavior is so like him. This tiny corner of cautious wisdom makes her heart leap.

"They holler at each other a lot," he says.

He's not walking down the aisle yet. Kate is not climbing out her bedroom window to elope either. They are just kids and, for the time being, they like that spot on her front-porch glider, the one that belonged to her grandmother. After all, the truth is: If you are a fifteen-year-old boy, one of life's fondest pleasures has to be unhooking the D-cup bra of a beautiful sixteen-year-old girl who thinks you are just the greatest, in spite of your braces and uncombed hair. She just has to be patient, let a certain modicum of real experience be his guide, and trust his instincts when it comes to this business of falling in love.

The Art of Reading Signals

The friend who related this story is an expert reader of her own boys' signals. Her two children are about two years apart in age and temperamentally dissimilar, despite having been raised in nearly identical surroundings and treated the same way, at the same time, by the same mom.

I know this can be true from my own experience parenting two children. From the very first day of life, Zach hated to close his eyes to go to sleep. Perhaps he was fearful that he might miss something. Meanwhile, Maggie, my daughter, slept so soundly and quietly as a newborn that we would check her breathing at night. My husband would put a butter knife under her tiny nose to make sure there were beads of moist respiration. What a sleeper, at least until she began to teethe! Zach still doesn't need much sleep. He'd rather be moving.

So what might account for one child's easy nature and the other's difficult temperament? As moms, we wonder: Is it us? Or is it him? Of course, it's both his nature and our nurturing. We can't help but react to our son's behavior. Sometimes he can't help acting on inherited aspects of his personality. Yet, says author Robert Karen in *Becoming Attached: The Unfolding Mystery of the Infant-Mother Bond and Its Impact on Later Life,* "No one knows for certain what the building blocks of temperament are." The link between heredity and behavior has been made by so many researchers that you can't ignore it. But you certainly aren't powerless here. You do have influence on the chemical broth (as psychologist Jerome Kagan describes it) of hormones, neurotransmitters, and peptides coursing through your son's brain.

Build on your intimate knowledge of your boy's inborn traits and try not to be too busy to read his signals.

Pick Up on Obscene Phone Calls

At about 3 A.M. on a September Sunday morning, the phone on her bedside table rings. Her boys, eighteen and sixteen, are sound asleep in their own beds down the hall, but she will soon check on them to make sure that much is still true. It's long after midnight, and anything could have happened in their social lives. Lying next to her husband, and now jolted from sleep, she and he both jump at the ringing. Who can this be so late? An emergency? These are the kinds of dark-night emotional rides we all dread, don't we? Her parents aren't well. Her husband's father has just had surgery for cancer. In the sandwich generation, caught between teenagers and elderly parents, they worry.

The caller's voice is young, masculine, and slightly familiar. What is he asking? Ick. Let's not repeat the litany of obscene, pornographic suggestions and words she is being given: pussy; blow job. There's a "suck" in there somewhere as well. You want to say, "Excuse me, what did you just say to me?" But you don't always have presence of mind in these situations. Is this caller alone? No, she can hear others. Young voices and laughter in the background make her even more alert. How gross.

She hangs up.

The phone rings again, within seconds. Once is not enough? How stupid. It's the same voice. A dimwit, he's either the ringleader or the poor dolt being prodded into making a fool of himself. Then she thinks of that redial option on everyone's phone now. Could this idiot have pressed her number accidentally a second time? Telephones offer so many options nowadays, even the opportunity to make the same mistake twice.

She hangs up again and puts on her glasses to check the caller ID. The number looks like a cell phone, if the area code is any indication. This kid is going to pay for his mistake. Thorough but not vindictive, my friend is the kind of person who never fails to complete a project. There's nothing unfinished in her home or her life. She will finish up this business of her obscene caller, one way or another.

Now she can't get back to sleep. Is this someone her sons know? Awake for the next thirty minutes, she promises herself she will find out who he is and do something about it in the morning. "It's okay," she tells her husband, who has settled back onto the pillow and is thinking about trying to get back to sleep. He looks angry and concerned for her. "I feel a little creepy but I'll be okay," she says. She knows boys pretty intimately, and she knows where their anxieties and hormones can take them. Still, boys who make obscene phone calls to someone's mother have loose screws that ought to be tightened by someone, she thinks. This kid needs to be straightened out. And, here's the real laugh: What kind of a goofball makes obscene (supposedly anonymous?) calls in an age of caller ID? He's left a telephone trail clearly marked for anyone, even her, to follow.

"I'll take care of it in the morning," she says. "Let's just hope the jerk doesn't dial us again."

Early the next day, she punches in the number the caller used and discovers that the cell phone belongs to a dad she knows from the lacrosse team meetings. This was no dad's voice, however. The home number is listed on one of her team rosters; she waits until just a little after 9 A.M. to call the family. A woman answers.

"Hi, my name is . . ." she begins, feeling a little uncomfortable because of the awkward accusation she's conveying and her unfamiliarity with this family. They've always been a little stiff at school gatherings.

Immediately, there is an uncomfortable sigh on the other end of the line.

"Oh no. Not you too?" this mother responds, cutting her off before she can even finish the explanation for her call.

My friend is taken aback and says, "What do you mean?" How could this woman know what she was calling about before she had barely opened her mouth?

"You are the eleventh mother to call, and I am so embarrassed. Did you get an obscene call last night?"

"Yes, I did," she says. "Two, in fact."

"Oh God. I am sorry. Really, really sorry. The boys were sleeping in my basement and had borrowed my husband's cell phone to order pizza, or so they said. I am so terribly embarrassed. We confronted them this morning. I don't think it was actually our son who was on the phone but there is still no excuse for any of this."

The boys, however, had refused to reveal the caller's identity. She had a pretty good idea who the culprit was, but my friend was curious and decided to dig a little deeper on her own.

"I know most of these boys," she tells me later, relating the tale, "and I couldn't help but replay the lines this creep used on me. It was a pretty harsh verbal assault, and I didn't like it one bit. This wasn't the kind of thing my own boys would have been involved in, and I knew they were both sound asleep at the time because I checked on them before I fell back to sleep."

She starts to have a little fun. On the way home from a tennis match later on that Sunday afternoon, she spots a group of familiar boys walking along Park Street and stops her car.

"Hey, guys, would you like a ride?" she asks. There are four of them.

Sure. They know her well and have spent time in her basement as well as the one from which the prank calls emanated.

Start with the chitchat. You do that so well. Smile easily. Go into your affectionate-mother mode. The boys don't suspect a thing and probably can't even remember if she was one of the moms on their obscene phone call hit list.

"How's school going?" she asks.

These boys in her car sense no signs of impending attack. They are kind of sleepy from the long night.

"Fine, fine," one or two or them answer. Someone hates the new geometry teacher. Another wishes he hadn't opted for Advanced Placement history. A nonconfrontational conversation begins.

"I've got way too much reading. It's going to kill me when ice hockey season starts," she hears from the backseat.

They aren't expecting her next move: a direct attack. "So which one of you called me a slut last night? Pussy? Asked for a blow job? C'mon, you can tell me."

There's quiet shock in the car.

"Spit it out, now. Who was it? I need to know."

After a chorus of protests, the kids give up the name of the culprit, who has already gone home. Trapped uncomfortably in her car, it seems they will do anything to wiggle off this hook. So much for loyalty to their good buddy. Turns out that he had been picked up earlier so he would be in time for church.

"Church?" She laughs. Her amazement and her smirk break the cool, guilty tension that has built up in the car's breathing space. "Well, isn't that funny? That's a good place for him to be this morning, don't you think?" They join her laughter.

"Didn't you guys even consider the idiocy of making obscene calls in an age of *caller ID*?"

Silence.

"I heard you all laughing in the background. He's not the only guilty party. Maybe he's just the dumbest."

They have arrived at a stoplight uptown, just doors down from the bagel shop, and the boys insist on exiting the car en masse.

"It was so funny," she recalls. "I didn't really intend to jerk them around so violently, but I guess I was really angry about the call, and they were so easy to catch. It just came naturally." She laughs. "You know, if I had set out to seek revenge or set them straight, it might never have happened. The situation just landed right there in my lap. As it was, I smiled all the way home after dropping them off."

The next afternoon, a Monday, when she arrives home from work about 4:30 P.M., her front door bell rings, offering another golden opportunity. Her younger son and a few friends are already in the basement, engrossed in some game on the PlayStation. Now, here in the flesh, on her doorstep, is the obscene caller with the ugly voice from very early Sunday morning.

"I was actually a little unnerved when I first saw him," she tells me. "He really does have quite a pornographic imagination for a kid. And I would never have expected him to show up so soon to face me when he *knew* that I *knew* who he was. Can you imagine the gall of this guy?" she asks me. I can't.

He smiles (seriously, he smiled!) and asks if her son is home.

"Yes, he is," she answers, without moving from the doorway. There is nothing welcoming in her body language or gestures.

"Can I come in?" he asks finally.

"No, in fact, you can't come in," she replies.

He looks surprised. She has always been one of those nice, accommodating moms.

"You aren't welcome in my house," she says. "I know it was you who made that obscene call to me."

Silent for a long minute, he says, "Well, I never thought you'd get so bent out of shape about it."

This big, brainless galumph of a guy is so amazingly naive and offensive at the same time that she can hardly believe her ears.

"How could you think that I wouldn't be bent out of shape?" she says, slamming the door in his face. When she looks out the window a few minutes later, he's still on the front step. Crazy kid.

"He's a jerk, Mom," her son says when she tells him who was just at the door. "He'll do anything for a laugh." So it was just a laugh that she and the ten other moms were trashed by his ugly words.

Maybe she should call his mother. Then again, maybe not.

Looking out the front window at the big boy now heading down the street, she hopes that his own mother is picking up on problems. This kid is sure sending signals that he needs a bit of parental intervention. The truth, she knows, is that her little bit of revenge may taste sweet, but prank callers are seeking more than the attention of the voice on the end of the line. She doesn't need any more to satisfy her appetite.

The Art of Making Mistakes

I used to write a newsletter for emergency room personnel on the topic of time. The publisher was anxious to reach time-starved ER doctors and nurses for advertising purposes, which is why the project was born. Eventually the publication died, which saddened me, because in the process of exploring all kinds of time-related topics in order to fill eight pages of editorial features three times a year, I met such a wide range of experts, on everything from yoga to physics. Management consultant Michael LeBoeuf, a retired university professor in Arizona, was one of my favorite sources for stories about understanding time. LeBoeuf had the ability to speak and write in snappy, insightful zingers, the kind of witty sayings you wanted to hold on to forever. Perhaps one of the wisest pronouncements he ever made, which goes straight to the heart of this mom's funny faux pas, was: "The worst mistake you can make is to become overly concerned with making mistakes."

There is no such place as perfection in parenting. In fact, trying to be perfect will make your son uncomfortable around you. You're human. Admitting your mistakes will also teach him how to forgive and forget. Psychologist Robert Karen, author of *The Forgiving Self: The Road from Resentment to Connection*, says, "Sometimes we get insight into our parents... and see how hard it is to get the job right." In this story, a thirteen-year-old learns a bit about his mother and also his dead father.

Check Your Assumptions

Imagine raising four teenage boys on your own without even the mixed blessing of a divorced mate somewhere in the wings. Her husband died when their youngest was just turning thirteen, and that experience, coupled with the weight of her worry about each one of her boys, colors lots of memories from those first years of parenting on her own. It was hard but funny at times. She recalls an occasion when the boys telephoned a restaurant where she was dining with a date. This was before the cell phone era. Near the end of the meal, the waiter alerted her to a phone call. She could take it up front.

"One of the kids," she explains, "was calling to reassure me that everything was okay now." When she asked what he meant by okay *now*, wondering, of course, what had not been okay in the hour she had just missed, since leaving on her first date in years, her son said, "Oh, the fire department has just left. It's out." Aw Mom, one of her boys had set the top kitchen cabinets on fire when he abandoned a bagel, which got stuck in the toaster that sat on her countertop, just beneath the cupboard.

Thank God, his older brother caught a whiff of the smoke and called 911 right away.

"What was funny," she recalls, "is the way the younger one delivered the line of explanation to me in the restaurant. Oh boy, was I mad at them, but just for a while. Anyone can make mistakes, and really the toaster was at fault. It should have popped up."

What also brings a smile to her face is the *Playboy* magazine incident.

Her husband had been dead for a short while when the youngest decided to move his bedroom upstairs to the attic, next to a storeroom on the third floor of their big old house. This boy accomplished the transition almost single-handedly, and she was happy about it because so much junk was discarded in the process. In this rite of passage, a step away from his big brothers in their second-floor bedrooms, he cast off some of his old toys, games, and boxes of papers from elementary school. She was also happy because she planned to convert his old bedroom into office space for herself. Those were months in which she was determined to bring order to her existence.

"The move was a good idea," she recalls. "I saw him in a different place emotionally, and he was also getting away physically from his brothers, who were already socializing, dating, and partying at fifteen, seventeen, and nineteen. In fact, my eldest had been away at college in New England but was taking a year at home and going to classes as a visiting student at a nearby college because of his father's death. Anyway, the older boys would bother and tease my youngest. By moving upstairs, he could play in peace, I thought. He was still just a kid and had taken his dad's death hard."

On this particular Saturday morning in October, he is not upstairs playing but at soccer practice. She's trying to organize her new home office and heads for the third-floor storeroom to retrieve something. That's when she spies them: piles and piles of *Playboy* magazines stashed in a corner.

"I freaked," she says. "I was furious and assumed they had emerged from his big cleanup but that he was too attached to part with them. I didn't even think he was all that interested in girls yet. My God, he still played with Legos! He didn't need *Playboy.*"

Her son arrives home from soccer practice at lunch and she's waiting for him.

"Let's go upstairs," she insists. "I have something to show you." He can tell she is angry and disappointed by something he's done but nothing in his conscience emerges as guilty. So they march up three flights and down the hall to the storage room. Inside, she points to the *Playboy*s.

"What are you doing with all these magazines?"

"Mom!" He's wearing a look of real, honest surprise, not guilt.

"I am so disappointed in you. I know you may be curious, but these are not real women," she protests.

"Mom!" He doesn't know what else to say.

"I want to know where you got them all."

"Mom!"

"You can tell me. Did one of your brothers pass them along?"

"Aw Mom. No, no."

"What?" she says. Then, "What?" again.

He answers, but slowly: "They're not mine. They belonged to Dad."

Quiet. "Who?"

"Dad," he replies.

"They did?" she asks.

"They did. We all knew they were here."

"You did."

"Of course."

"Oh. Oh my. I didn't," she admits.

"I could hardly believe it," she tells me later. "Then we started laughing. He really was just still a *boy* who liked to *play*. That made me feel so stupid. What a mistake."

We both start to laugh at her blunder as well as the variation on the word *playboy*.

Later, as she looks through the magazines, checking the publication dates on the old issues, she wonders what else she never knew about the man she had loved. And why, for heaven's sake, had he chosen to save all the magazines. A legacy for his sons?

"What a riot," she says. "Such a male thing, don't you think? Each one of the boys had known about the stash of girlie magazines their dad kept up there. I had been the only one left out of the loop but in a way, my mistake opened up a whole new line of private laughter among us at a time that was so important. It was good for us to joke about it. We still laugh whenever we think of *Playboy* today."

The truth is: sons who grow up in less than perfect households, where mothers do make mistakes and can laugh about their errors, may be better prepared to cope with the pressures of the adult world later on. So try not to beat yourself up too much.

The Art of Being
His Secret Weapon

Anthropologist Margaret Mead once said that every child needs someone to remember what happened to him yesterday. I know this directive sounds simpleminded, but it is definitely not. Think about it: When a good friend remembers that you were at your wit's end yesterday and asks how you are today, you feel validated, don't you? Mentally, we moms often hold on to bits and pieces of our sons' lives. Occasionally, I'd like my brain to stop, just stop doing this. It can get crowded in there, and being able to focus on one thing at a time is a relief. But you can't do that with boys, can you? And these pieces of young life that we hold aren't inconsequential. Your awareness of his fear, his failure, his success, whether it be that winning goal or that flunked biology test, makes you a very powerful weapon in his arsenal.

The American Heritage Dictionary offers more than

one definition for the word *armor*: "1. A defensive covering, such as chain mail, worn to protect the body. 2. A tough protective covering. 3. Something serving as a safeguard or protection." At first I thought only one of these explanations shed light on this mom's story. He was *arming* himself for school and adolescent social encounters through his appearance and his demeanor. Then I looked again and saw how each definition could apply to each of them—not just the part about "defensive covering." "Something serving as a safeguard or protection" certainly suits this particular mom.

Recognize His Armor

He has been growing and cultivating dreadlocks for months and months. His hair looks positively wicked to her, and someone recently offered her a scientific interpretation of what exactly goes into building these long, sticky dreadlocks. (He certainly doesn't wash his hair the way he once did.)

"I try not to say much about it," she admits, "because I sense he's okay on so many other levels. His hair is not a battle I want to pick." However, the two rings in his eyebrow and the one in his tongue, which she recently discovered, do worry her.

"What kind of statement is he trying to make here?" she asks me. "Where did he get the money for this?" She knows about the girl on the next street whose tongue became pus-filled with infection, but she was never privy to what exactly happened in the aftermath. By the way, he also wears the crotch of his baggy pants at knee level and sports a chain that loops from a saggy pocket to a belt loop.

This mother and I are talking at the high school. My lame response: "Who knows? They are all so different." (Secretly, I'm pleased that I never had to deal with a tongue ring in either of my teenagers' mouths.) We know you just can't compare one boy to any other or to expect some norm to keep every son in line. We commiserate: Look t MTV; his role models aren't the kids we watched on *Father Knows Best* or even *The Wonder Years.* "It's tough being a teenager sometimes. Have you been caught in the hallway during the change of classes?" Perhaps public high school survival requires armor we never imagined.

Now she laughs. We are working side by side reading papers as volunteers at the local high school in the ninth-grade English program. The group of four or five meets most Friday mornings for first and second period, and the scene of sharing can become intimate and funny. We've been doing it all through the school year and now it's May.

"He tries so hard to be cool and tough and actually takes longer to get dressed than my daughter," she says. "The other morning before school, I saw him shoving a white shirt in his backpack and asked him what it was for."

"I'm playing Romeo today in Mr. A.'s class," he explains. For a second, she has to smile, thinking of him in this romantic role. He's fourteen.

"Who's Juliet?" she asks.

"This girl who is a real bitch," he replies.

"Oh, that's too bad," she says. "How do you know?"

"Well, yesterday when we were practicing, I touched her and she got pissed off. Jeez, Mom," he says, "she screamed so loud—'Get off my back you m——f——!'—that Mr. A., who never, ever gets upset or raises his voice, was furious."

"So are you nervous about today?" she asks him. By this time, they are in the car, heading for the high school drop-off circle.

"A little," he admits. "She's bigger than me, too." They were on a busy side street next to the school.

Seated at the table in the writers' room, his mother relates the story and asks us, the crew of regular volunteers, "Want to know what happened next?"

Of course.

"Well, you know that you don't dare touch them in semi-public places," she says, "but as he went to exit the car, I patted his knee. I was worried about him and the Romeo role he'd have to play with a bitchy Juliet. But he turned away quickly and opened the door.

"Think about this," she asks the group, "can you imagine how hard it is to exit a car gracefully when the crotch of your pants is at your knees? He was in such a hurry to get away from me that as he put his right leg out on the curb and grabbed for the backpack, his chain got caught on something. I guess it was the seat lever. Who knows? But he fell right out the door and nearly lost his pants. I felt so bad for him but I almost laughed, too. Isn't that awful?"

A universal "Aaaaawwww" is heard around the table of volunteers. Some of us have sons, too. Though we don't mind volunteering in the high school, there isn't one among us who would want to go back to being a student there. We'd need more than dreadlocks to survive. We'd probably need a full suit of armor out there.

"I didn't move," she says, "though I considered getting out of the driver's seat to see if he was okay. The fact that this was at 8 A.M. and the sidewalks were crowded with kids made me think twice about acting like a mother. He would have been mortified."

We agreed. He recovered quickly, but she thought about her Romeo all morning long and during his scheduled lunch, she beeped him. (Of course, he has a beeper and cell phone.

Doesn't everyone?) When he picked up the page a little later, she could tell he was purposely adjusting his voice to a surreptitious purr.

"Hey, Mom," he whispers secretively. Is that a hand cupped over his mouth?

"Are you okay?" she asks.

"Sure."

"How did your Shakespeare scene go?" Don't ask about bruises or bumps from the fall.

"Really good," he says. Relief on her end, but there's a bit of surprise, too. "I had to help her with her lines a little but she didn't call me a m—— f——" he adds. They laugh.

"Gotta go," he says quickly, but the slight shift in his voice to an upper level lets her know that he is happy she called. It seems that *she* can still make him feel safe, protected, and tougher than he really is.

The truth is, she loves this part of her job description. For the rest of a perfectly ordinary afternoon filled with chores, her mind kept returning to his positive feedback. She'd even break into a ridiculous smile, thinking of how good she felt about the way his day spun forward successfully when it had begun so ominously with the spill onto the sidewalk in front of school. For her, that little lift in his voice on the phone tasted as sweet as his baby kisses once did. And though he may arm himself using clothing, piercings, and monosyllabic answers as he successfully pulls away from her, she also knows he still needs her on occasion. Forget the hair and the big chain . . . *she* may be the best secret weapon in his life.

The Art of Manipulation

New research about how brains grow and change during various points in life indicates that middle-aged women have more in common with their teenage sons than anyone imagined. Seriously. You need myelin, a fatty coating on your brain's nerve cells, in order to make cognitive connections. Harvard Medical School psychiatrist Francine M. Benes, M.D., Ph.D., has shown that teenagers experience a 100 percent jump in myelination—the building up of the myelin coating in your brain. The surprise is that in midlife, as you inch toward fifty, to be exact, you are the beneficiary of a second huge jump, or 50 percent more, myelin in your brain. I like to think of my brain as laying down new and circuitously different pathways.

Maybe the myelination taking place helps explain why mothers and sons can be equally skilled in manipulation. Doesn't the art of manipulation make you think of plots, subplots, twists, and turns in a story? Think of manipulation as a loaded term that can be okay in practice. No one likes the idea of being manipulated, but if it's for good reasons, why shouldn't we moms exercise our options?

Share the Past

Her two-story house is set back from the road by tall trees and beautiful landscaping. She and her husband live in an old section of town. The front door is not in the front but on the side, opening to the long driveway. Tonight, or should I say this morning, she becomes very slowly aware of a red light casting a strange, beating-heart glow into her bedroom window. The clock on the bedside table shows 2:12 A.M. She shakes her husband awake because the doorbell is ringing.

One son is away at lacrosse camp, but the oldest, who is sixteen, is asleep down the hall. Pulling her bathrobe from the closet hook, trying to find her way into the sleeves in the dark, she races down to answer the door. Her hardworking husband follows in his pajamas. An executive with a major pharmaceutical company, he has kept working hours that have been insane recently. Happily married, she's been parenting her boys for years. She's good at it. And her husband is good at keeping his cool and his life to himself. Being pulled from the warmth of bed is not his thing at all.

At the door, a young police officer asks, "Do you know where your son is?"

"Of course, he's sleeping upstairs," they both answer in unison.

"Are you sure? Asleep?"

Behind the officer, in the backseat of that official car with its blinking lights, is a face they recognize. He's a friend of their sons. Hmmm. Sleepyheaded, they are directed outside into the night air onto the stone veranda and motioned to look over at the side of their own house. There's a ladder positioned near an open bedroom window.

Burglar? Hardly. In the open frame is their sixteen-year-old, obviously caught in the act.

"From what this fella tells me," the officer says pointing a finger at the kid in the car, "I think they were planning a run to the local Dunkin' Donuts. I followed him for several blocks carrying his ladder. I think he was afraid we were going to book him on attempted burglary. That's why he felt compelled to give up the identity of his escape artist partner in crime up there."

They all look up at the window again. He nods but doesn't dare indicate any interest in coming down.

"I'm going to give this guy a ride home now but I wonder if you could arrange for the return of the ladder tomorrow?" He points to the boy in the car. "He says it came from his parents' garage."

"Oh sure. No problem," her husband says, smiling.

As they walk back into the house and close the front door, she says, "You know that there are doughnuts in the kitchen."

"They just don't taste the same as the ones he might have been eating by now," her husband admits. That icing of danger and thrill of adventure are delicious when you are sixteen.

"You're right," she says, smiling. "I wonder what he's thinking up there." There has been no sign that he plans to emerge from his bedroom and come down the staircase inside. All is quiet on that front.

"Let's let him wonder what we have planned as punishment. I don't even want to know if that's what they were really up to," she says.

"Sure you don't want to talk to him tonight?" her husband asks.

"It can wait until the morning. In fact, silence is on our side tonight," she says, adding, "Have you ever told him about the time you and your friends broke into the Post Road pool and got caught by the cops?"

"Nah."

"You should," she suggests.

She shakes her head. She knows that story well. It was part of both their pasts because they have been together since high school. Maybe it's time for him to tell their son.

"Take him out for doughnuts," she suggests. "Let him in on what you were like as a sixteen-year-old. After spending the night stewing fearfully, he may enjoy knowing he's not the first in his family to have had a close encounter with the law in the middle of the night."

The truth is, these two men in her life need to know a lot more about each other. While she'd like to shirk the responsibility for getting them together, she won't. Her power over both of them is significant. Sure, she can become angry with her husband for not realizing his worth as a father. Bitching about what he doesn't do for his sons or how often he isn't around is not going to help anyone, however. She also knows that for generations, men were not encouraged to be hands-on caregivers—that was society's dictate. But not anymore. Even now that so many guys have been diving into fathering seriously, on occasion it still takes a bit of manipulation to show them which opportunities for intimacy are worth grabbing. Manipulation has several meanings, of course, but the one she chooses to savor is "to control by skill . . . to influence or manage shrewdly." She smiles, thinking of herself as shrewd. That's a nice adjective.

The Art of Practicality

I used to work for *Ladies' Home Journal*, which still bears that wonderful slogan, "Never underestimate the power of a woman." In my early twenties I sat at a junior editor's desk there in the 1970s, opening slush mail, going to meetings, and editing articles full of practical advice about dieting (which lived side by side editorially with decadent chocolate cake recipes. So much for logic, huh?). And, of course, there were parenting pieces, too. From this three-decade distance, I laugh about some of our how-to lessons for mothers, especially now that I have a bit of practical distance as a mother myself. Remember, those were the pre–Martha Stewart days. But we certainly weren't slouches in our efforts to empower women to make use of all their talents.

Actually, I remember treasuring those buzzwords about not underestimating our female instincts. Some very practical mothers, like the one in this story, are instinctively aware of what needs to be done and how to make use of objects that ought to be discarded— even when it comes to managing the murky waters of drinking during adolescence. These are the scary years, when binge drinking can become a rite of passage and competitive event. All sons, mothers, and families are different, with a wide range of social mores. Personally, you may need to rely on a strict set of guidelines for what's never acceptable behavior and actually cause for alarm. Teenage abuse of alcohol can be a very dangerous game indeed. Yet, in this boy's case, and with his mother's no-nonsense practicality, it didn't turn out that way.

Be Ready for Beer Bongs

He is seventeen. You don't need to know her age. She could be you because she is the mother of a nice, intelligent, attractive, curious, fearless, big boy. He has moved his bedroom to the basement of their pretty three-story suburban New Jersey home because his older sister took over the attic the year before. Two of the bedrooms on the second floor are unoccupied now except for drop-in visitors because of this search for separate personal space. This doesn't bother her at all. In fact, it's quite nice for her and her husband to have the floor to themselves when the lights go out.

All the kids in town know his room well. It's tucked into a nice basement, down the back steps from the kitchen and opposite the laundry area. Believe me, this is no dark dungeon. You can even see out the windows. With the help of his parents, he has outfitted his white-walled, gray-tiled area with a black leather wraparound couch, two chairs, an enormous, odd-angled coffee table, carved from the trunk of a tree and lacquered, weighing a ton (purchased at a yard sale, courtesy of his dad's aberrant taste), a desk, his computer, and two single beds—one for a friend whose family has moved out of town and left him behind to complete the school year. Blue and white banners, "Most Improved Player" plaques, and a collection of ice hockey and lacrosse trophies testify to his calm, cool athletic presence on any team. You want this guy on your side to score that last goal, take the only shot possible, date your daughter. Speaking of shots, commemorative shot glasses, Mardi Gras beads, now empty beer, Absolut, and Cutty Sark bottles, and an official "Beirut Champion 2000" (with a Ping-Pong ball stuck to a defiant metallicized plastic arm) speak of other high points in a high school life . . . and I do want you to put the emphasis on *high*.

But he's a good kid, she says. He's the one who collects the car keys at a party, never failing to call her for a ride home from anywhere, anytime. "Oh God, I've even been a getaway driver unknowingly when the police raided a graduation party. For heaven's sake, I wasn't trying to escape. They hopped in and said, 'Let's go, Mom.' " She knows him well. She doesn't approve of underage drinking but she doesn't condemn it either. He has room to grow, she believes.

Early one Sunday morning in August, she finds a purple funnel about six inches in diameter, with a two-foot-long clear plastic, retractable tube attached. It's sitting in her laundry sink. Smells like beer. The boys are still asleep behind his bedroom door. Will be for hours. "I knew it wasn't good, and this thing definitely looked like something for one of their drinking games, so I decided to take it." Having confiscated contraband before, she surmised that the boys would never consciously seek her input about its whereabouts. They wouldn't dare, but neither would she use it as an opportunity to confront, embarrass, or punish. Not her style. End of conversation. End of story. But not really. Rather than toss the found treasure right then, she shoved it into a cupboard with some other tools in the storage room next to his bedroom, right there in the basement. Quietly, they probably looked for it for months, she admits. Hee-hee.

When Christmas comes and the tree goes up, the first time she is forced to get on her knees and climb under the branches to fill the basin with water, she has a great idea. Where was that funnel? At first she couldn't remember where she had put the thing. You always think you are going to remember exactly where you store infrequently used items but the next time someone with a bowl of unshelled walnuts asks for your nutcracker, your memory is anything but clear. In this case, it all comes back to her. Downstairs, second shelf, in the storage room. With a length of wire from the same cabinet, she attaches the funnel to the trunk of the Christmas tree, carefully snaking its tube straight down and into the top of the tree stand. Nice. Now she can water daily with no need for any sort of floor-level gymnastics or reaching through unopened gifts and low-lying boughs of evergreen. "I always hated watering the tree. It was great because I could just stand and water. I didn't have to go under," she says. Even the purple color at the heart of the tree wasn't so bad, when viewed all together with the ornaments and lights.

He doesn't notice it at first, and she doesn't point out her invention either. Then it happens. A glimpse of purple; a flash of recognition.

"Aw Mom. You didn't."

"I did," she hollers from the kitchen.

He's not laughing yet. Later his friends come over for her Christmas cookies and good laughs about the new life of their beer bong.

When a picture of him with the end of the beer bong tube in his mouth is discovered in a pile of summer snapshots, he shows her how it's really supposed to be used.

"I like my idea better," she says.

With that, a thought occurs to her that other mothers might need a tree bong, too. Can she package it? Just how did that mother and daughter who made a financial killing on those white icicle Christmas lights last year get started?

"Aw Mom, don't go there."

Jokes are being made all the time about how Martha Stewart can practically turn trash into treasure. But how many moms do you know who are able to turn an illegal beer bong into both a practical joke and a legitimate practical use?

The Art of Listening

For several years I worked alongside a mother of ten. Yes, I said ten children. I mentioned Kay Willis in the Introduction, but having six girls in a row and then four boys makes her story important enough to be continued here. She was funny, wise, and one of the best listeners I ever encountered. She used to say things like, "Try to remember: God gave you two ears and only one mouth, so listen twice as much as you talk." Moms can become good at criticizing, instructing, correcting, and worrying about sons, especially during their teen years. For good reason, of course, because boys are so notoriously gifted at not really thinking before acting and we fear they might kill themselves or someone else, to be frank. Yet, Kay would insist, "Listening—not criticizing, instructing, correcting—may be the more important part of all conversations with kids."

Unfortunately, there are so many obstacles along the way to becoming good listeners. If you are like me, you are really busy, unable to set aside other thoughts, and not always present even when your son is around. Let's put it this way: Think about how rejected you feel when you are trying to talk to someone who is obviously not listening to you. To be a good listener, you've got to be open-minded, a state that seems to be increasingly rare in our fast-paced social milieu. On the other side of this listening dilemma is the son who has learned not to listen to you and has pretty much closed his mind to you. That's tough.

For me, one of the most productive opportunities for communicating is over the phone. There must be something about the voice-only connection that is unthreatening and comforting. Find your own special places to talk. My neighbor used to love long car rides, for example. In this story, a little bit of danger helped close a gap in the conversation between a mother and son.

Stay Close

He is going to turn eighteen, which is really hard to believe. Quietly, without making very many waves in her household, he has reached a point from which she doesn't expect him to return to her, though this is not an angst- or anger-riddled story. She loves him but wonders what he is thinking most of the time. He has a comfortable attitude with adults and easy-going good looks, so he slides out of most sticky situations without even breathing deeply or letting her know he's been stuck. He is just so closemouthed about his affairs . . . usually.

He loves cars, works part-time at an auto repair/sales/

detailing shop, and is attending the local community college. On this particular day, he and a co-worker are delivering a distinctive black Mercedes to its owner down the interstate, several towns away.

His three younger sisters have been much more forthcoming with her, and her first observation as she begins to share a high-speed-chase story is that "getting information about boys is tough because getting information out of boys is tough." We moms can almost all agree to that. It can take a nightmare for some boys to spill the beans about what they've been thinking.

She knows so much more about what goes on in her girls' lives than she ever did with this boy. He doesn't want to listen to her very much anymore. He is the oldest. Her girls have always sounded their emotional alarms loud and clear. Big deals about issues hardly ever even make it onto his radar screen. He keeps her in the dark a lot. Take proms, for example. The daughter just behind this laid-back boy required hours of motherly investment in the dress, the date, the hair, the limo, who's going with whom and who wasn't going with whom. The night before the big event, she finds out her son was going too. His khaki pants were clean and, yes, there was a pressed blue shirt in her husband's closet. She made a quick trip to the florist and arrived back right before he drove off to pick up his date. Who was she? "I didn't know," she admits. When she asked him what color the date's dress was, he didn't know. She adds, "I picked a white corsage."

The only articles of dress he cares deeply about are his jeans and what he puts on his feet. You can call them sneakers if you want, but owning these latest versions of athletic footgear take you far beyond the canvas Keds in feel or financial terms. "He wants to be able to tie these sneakers once and never again," she explains, "so they can become slip-ons," calling for no bending, no wasted consumption of exertion or time that could be spent sleeping. "I buy two pairs of expensive, name-brand shoes and he is set for a season. With my girls, quantity counts. The right color, the right heel, the right look, you know," she says. She goes to Payless or can shop discount, but he wants quality because he doesn't like his feet to hurt. "This is a comfort thing," she says, something women don't seem to understand or if we do, we don't care about it when we are young.

She does try to keep the lines of communication open, watching and waiting for opportunities. She had been thinking about how funny it is that she knows he's having sex. "He won't wear the white cotton underpants I buy in the grocery store in six-packs anymore," she explains. "They must have a designer label now. He's also been doing small loads of his own laundry. Supposedly he's saving me the hassle, but I know he's protecting his private life."

Her suspicions were confirmed when she found two used condoms in his bedroom wastebasket. She and her husband had spent a long Saturday away at a wedding and all three of his sisters had been dropped off with friends for the day. Left to his own devices—to use that word more than just figuratively—he took advantage of the privacy. On one hand, she is dismayed. Then, on the other hand, both she and his dad are delighted that he has used protection. Ultimately hysterical, they laugh at the idea of him putting this evidence into his bedroom wastebasket. Who does he think empties the trash? A maid? Ha! Him? Not a chance. It's the path-of-least-resistance mentality at work in his world once again. In case you are wondering, she decided that her husband should speak with him about sex in his bedroom. If he's making these kinds of decisions, then he'd better be prepared to handle any consequences. They aren't ready to be grandparents and he's not ready to handle fatherhood on his own anytime soon. "With boys, you've gotta be simple and direct," she says. You've also gotta be in the right place at the right time to hear them.

On this day, she's at her desk in the office, not too busy to talk to him.

The phone rings. She answers.

Try to picture him now, the quiet, monosyllabic son, telling this story: He's on the interstate in his own car, following his buddy from the car detail shop, who is in the black Mercedes up ahead. They are having fun tailgating. He stays close because after his friend delivers the car they have been detailing at the garage where they both work, he can drive him back. He knows what he's doing. Done this a dozen times already.

Coming into a crowded merge point, he reaches down to put in a new CD. When he looks up, he spots the Mercedes just as it starts to exit the highway. So soon. He thought they had a few more exits to go. Crossing lanes of heavy traffic, he manages to catch up and follows for miles and miles until the driver speeds up and circles around and around the same block several times, then races into a driveway, jumps out, and runs into a house. The problem is, this driver is not his co-worker but a frightened woman who happens to have been driving the same model black Mercedes. He had been following the wrong car.

Before he can escape, a man (probably the driver's husband) comes racing out of the front door with something in his hand—a gun?—and two really big dogs. Her son had pulled up in the suburban driveway behind the Mercedes, and now he can't back out fast enough. His wits betray him. Fumbling to open the driver's-side window (is it bulletproof?) to explain, he gasps, "I'm sorry. It was a mistake," while throwing the car into reverse. The guy is racing toward him. With heart pounding wildly, he slams the car back and around and manages to peel screeching down the quiet side street in a neighborhood of confusing cul-de-sacs and endless circles.

Whatever happened to grids and cross streets that make numerical and logical sense? He's lost. He's afraid.

Breathing hard, looking in his rearview mirror to see if the husband is in pursuit, he is really scared. There is no one back there. He breathes a little easier. This is crazy. There is his cell phone. Pick it up. Call someone. Checking his calls, he realizes his buddy has tried to reach him not once but three times. But before he can call anyone, his phone goes dead. Damn. Dumb battery.

Circling. Circling. He gets himself really lost for at least another thirty or forty minutes before finding a gas station and getting directions back to the interstate.

How does she know all the intricate, intimate details of this story? Well, when he is finally back to civilization and can get to a pay phone, she is the first person he calls.

She can tell by his tone of voice that he's not all right.

"What's happened?"

"My heart is still beating so fast, Mom," he says, starting to explain his nightmarish afternoon ride.

She is so glad she was sitting still, that she answered her phone, that she was ready to listen, and, most important, that he called, offering the gift of emotion. "He was so afraid. It was as though he were three again and wanted to show me his skinned knee so I could make it better."

The truth is: even though your son may seem distant, he'll know whom to call, if you refuse to let go and you keep in touch.

The Art of Crying

Do you cry at weddings? Funerals? Sad movies? What kind of a crier are you? Do you cry at all? Have you watched Iraqi, Palestinian, Israeli, or Afghani mothers weep, wail, keen, moan, whimper, and sob publicly on news reports, expressing the grief, sorrow, and pain in their countries?

A good friend would often emerge from her car weeping on early mornings to meet me for tennis in Brookdale Park. Why was she crying? "The music," she would say, admitting that she had been touched to tears by a piece of music on her car radio. I'd laugh, but of course I loved the fact that her emotions were right there and so touchable. Yes, it's a good idea to dampen down some emotional edges so we can think clearly. You don't want your son to think you are emotionally unstable, of course. Tears can flood my ability to be rational, that's for sure. But, oh gosh, go ahead and let go on occasion. There is no crime in crying.

Don't Hide Raw Feelings

He's fifteen. She smiles now, remembering the night in May it happened. At the time, there was nothing even remotely amusing about it. She had cried, in public, in front of strangers, acting like a wimp. No other parent had broken down that way. That image, of the circle of concerned parents, comes back— among all the other dads gathered in the police station at midnight, only her husband saw the light of a little humor in the scene. Let me put you there now.

He is in tenth grade and for his birthday last month, a Mets game was the perfect ticket. He had loved it, almost catching a fly ball down the first-base line. He's the kind of kid who still takes a glove to a professional baseball game. Still a boy, learning how to shave this season, he's just a slightly bigger boy from last year at this time. His baseball cap? Well, it's a Mets cap and, frankly, she thinks of it as his most hole-y of holy hats. He wears it all the time, even through dinner if his dad doesn't make him take it off. She's been tempted to let it ride the top rack of her dishwasher to rid it of that sweaty head smell, but he loves it so much that she can't bear to imagine it being altered in any way. Occasionally, he still grabs her hand when they walk down a city street, but not when any of his buddies are around, and definitely not in their own town. Yes, sometimes he will just reach out, slip his hand into hers, and remind her of when he was little. This makes her feel absolutely wonderful, though perhaps a little wistful about letting go of the early years of mothering.

Though she fixates a bit about all the newfound freedom he's found in the daily business of school life with 2,400 students, she trusts him. He works hard, always has, and she also knows that his capacity to worry ranks right up there with hers. To picture him now, you can see in his demeanor the instinct to please adults. Is this respect for authority or is it fear? Whatever it is, ordinarily his caution makes her life as his mother easier than for most.

On a warm Friday evening, she asks him and four friends if they want to go to the movies. Her husband is playing poker with a group of guys from town, his once-a-year thing.

"No thanks, Mom," her son says.

The implication that these boys have better things to do is apparent. After all, this is a weekend night and they are still working on their game plan for this evening's action. Pizza uptown? A party somewhere? Somebody knows something, they hope. There's a sweet sixteen party at the Commonwealth Club nearby, though none of them has been invited. One thing is certain—as a group, they wouldn't dare be seen with somebody's mother and somebody's little sister.

"Do you have any money?" she asks him.

"No, can I have some?"

"Sure." Opening her pocketbook, retrieving a wallet, she pulls out a five-dollar bill. "Will this be enough?"

"I don't know what we are doing yet," he explains.

"Be careful. You can call your dad at the Metrigliosos' if you need a ride somewhere or anything else. He'll be there until at least eleven, I think. Here's the number," she says, writing it down for him.

"Okay. Don't worry."

The movie starts at 8:10 P.M., and it's still light out when she and her daughter back out of the driveway in the van.

"Are you sure you guys will be all right?" she hollers out the car window to them.

"Mom! Will you stop! We don't want to go with you."

Three hours later, no one is home when she and her daughter cross the back porch and step into the kitchen. All the lights are on. Just like him, she thinks, a little piqued that he will never flip the switch off. At least the back door was closed. There is no sign of him or his friends, and that's worrisome. They should be home by now. Her husband's car is still missing, too. Uh-oh. He's not much of a gambler, however. If he's lost money in the game, it's only pennies.

The light on the answering machine blinks the number 6. So many calls. Busy night. Better check. Wonder where her boy is? It's after eleven now. He knows he's supposed to phone home with his whereabouts. Maybe that's him on the machine. As she digs into her pocketbook searching for her little address telephone book to call other mothers and locate him, she pushes the play button.

The first voice landed on the tape at 9:45 P.M. A chorus of others had followed, but that first one is the killer. So deep and scary. Do they teach intonation in police academies? Her heart starts pounding. "This is Police Officer Michael Mazanata. We have your son in custody. . . . Please call . . ." Her son? In custody? The respectful kid in the hole-y Mets cap. Where? She plays the message back twice before dialing first her husband and then the number at the station. She needs directions and a city map because her child is two towns away in an urban lockup.

Fearful and furious, she does the driving. Her husband has had more than three beers and certainly doesn't want to risk a drunken driving citation on this kind of rescue mission. They've been given no official indication about why the boys were picked up or what charges might await. So she assumes the worst. Drinking? Doing drugs? What else could it be? Beer? Probably beer.

"I could kill him," she says. "I am so angry."

"Hold it. Hold on," her husband insists. "You don't know what happened."

"Oh, but I can imagine," she says. "Those boys are so stupid. So stupid."

Inside the station, she walks past a row of chairs, heading to the night desk, recognizing parents waiting their turn. Glancing over to the corner of the room, she spies a cage—yes, that's what it looks like—about six feet by six feet, with mesh wire extending from floor to ceiling. Inside are the boys, five of them. There isn't enough room to sit. They've been standing for hours and they look scared. Two have been crying. What is this? Her fury starts to dissipate. She starts to cry. Stalwart is not a word you would use to describe her emotional temperature, even though she'd like to retain her composure. The other parents in the police station don't want to follow her down that path, in fact. One father is visibly angry with his son and anchoring the blame for the evening squarely on his son's shoulders.

What have they done? The charges are curfew violation, not possession of alcohol, drugs, deadly weapons, or stolen goods. Curfew violation? Whose curfew? Not hers. How would she know that county parks have official curfews even on warm spring evenings? Tomorrow she will walk down to the sign at the official entrance to the park near their home where the boys were picked up. Let's see what the fine print on the welcome sign says. As the object of her anger shifts, the flush of tears is right there. Oh jeez. Does she have a tissue? Not now. Wait till you get in the car. Crying always makes her feel so powerless and so stereotypically female.

Unlocked from the cage, he is standing next to his dad now. He has put one arm around their son's shoulders. Both look serious. Nearly three decades of marriage have made it possible for her to pick up the scent of her husband's moods easily. She catches a whiff of amusement.

The boys had gone for a walk in the park, that's it.

"Really?" she asks in the car. "Is that all?"

Her husband is driving, quite sober now after the cold splash of the arrest and her quiet hysteria. Where do those tears come from? she wonders. Her sobs even caught her by surprise and forced the officer to stop in mid-sentence as he tried to explain how far this case would go.

Straining the seat belt strapped across her shoulder, she twists to face the back of the van, where he is slumped down, exhausted. Her face is wet, eyes puffy already. Tomorrow she will look ragged and red-eyed. Why is it that in the movies, heroines can cry and still look beautiful? There should really be an after-crying cosmetic available.

"Well, we heard there might be a party," he admits. "But Mom, this guy, this Mazanata, he was crazy."

"You shouldn't have been down there in the park," she argues. She's fingering the county police department arrest report and other paperwork nervously. "You could have gone to the movies with me."

"Mom, not anymore. We didn't want to do that. We had other things to do."

"Like this? Get arrested?"

Still light at 8:45 P.M., they realized that five bucks weren't enough for an entire pizza, so they headed for the park. Near the playground area, before they had a chance to find friends or action, a county police car caught sight of them strolling and sped right at them, across the grass, down the slope, through the trees, going really fast.

"Right onto the gravel near the swings!" he says. "We thought he was going to crash into that new jungle gym or go into the pond."

They ran. If you were a fifteen-year-old and a crazed cop car was heading straight at you, what would you do?

"Why did you run?" she asks.

"Because. Because. Well, just because. We were afraid."

"You looked guilty," she says. "Running made you look like you were guilty of something."

"I know. I know."

What a case of official police overkill, she thinks. He's been handcuffed, thrown into the back of a patrol car, taken on a high-speed ride through city streets, and locked in a cage for three hours.

"We kept slamming and sliding back and forth on the seat, Mom. We couldn't hold on and weren't in seat belts."

"The police car . . . was going that fast?" she questions.

"Ninety miles an hour!" he says. "I saw the speedometer, Mom. It was amazing. Just like in the movies. I wouldn't lie to you. That guy, Mazanata, was a crazy man." He pauses, uncertain whether to share the next piece.

"Did you see the woman he was talking to in the station? The one in the corner when you guys came in?"

"No. I don't think so."

"Well, he bragged to us that she was a whore and they were going out later. He was just waiting for you to get there. Then they were going to go . . . you know, Mom, they were going to go out. He was so stupid that when he asked me to describe what I was wearing when I was arrested, I told him it was a khaki jacket."

"What do you mean?" she asks, wondering where this line of rationale is going.

"Well, I didn't think he could spell *khaki*."

Home now, in the kitchen, she puts the police paperwork on the table to look for that word *khaki* under the box for *Scars, Marks and Other Descriptive Data Including Clothing Worn*.

There is no "khaki" jacket. The officer has written "tan" instead.

Down by *Signature of Person Juvenile Released To,* her husband has signed his name. She breathes a sigh of knowing, relieved that she can almost always count on him for things like this when times are tough, even after a night of poker and beer. Turning the focus on her own behavior, she's frustrated. Why does she have to be so emotional? Crying at the sight of her son in that cage. Ugh. She wishes she could be stronger, but when it comes to her mothering, raw feelings are the rule. This is her baby, her little boy not really grown up yet and thrust into such a stressful situation for no good reason. In the end, all the police could come up with was curfew violation.

"Why don't you go on upstairs to bed. I'll be right up to tuck you in," she says to her fifteen-year-old. His face looks white. He's worried. "Do you think I'll have a police record because of this?" he asks. "What about my college applications? Tim says you can't lie on them and this will show up." Friend Tim had been in the cage with him.

"We'll talk to Uncle Tom. We can figure this out." Her brother is a lawyer.

Before turning out the light, looking back at the yellow copy of the arrest report one more time, she notices box #34, in a long list of questions her son was asked by the arresting officer. This one calls for *Name and Address of Next of Kin,* and is just below the line with the "tan" jacket. She giggles about this "khaki" versus "tan" question. Her son is such a naturally good speller. So is she. Expecting to see her husband's name in that next of kin slot, a slow jolt of deep down intimate knowledge about herself and her son hits her.

It's her name she sees in the box. Yes, that's her name, spelled nearly correctly. She starts to cry again for the second time this evening, realizing how centrally located she is in this boy's psyche: the first person in his mind for a rescue when he's in danger: "Me, his mother," she says to her husband, who is smiling, too. "Wimpy me."

Yes, there is an art to crying while still holding on to your power. Don't be embarrassed. Some mothers have nearly perfected it.

The Art of
Getting Rid of Guilt

....

"Growth in awareness is painful," Anne Morrow Lindbergh writes in *A Gift From the Sea*. Believe me, nothing hurts more than an eye-opening window into your son's life that spotlights something missing in your mothering. Guilt is such a universal emotion for mothers. It descends upon you in the delivery room and is reinforced everywhere you turn. Even a casual comment from a stranger can send guilty shivers down your spine. When Zach was a four-year-old at the nursery school across the street from our house, he spent a couple of weeks wearing all his favorite T-shirts with numbers on the front at the same time. This might mean he'd sit in class with up to nine tees layered on each other. Yes, he looked a bit bulky, but I just smiled quietly to myself. He was quite serious about his numbers. To show them off, he'd proudly pull them up individually and count off.

One day another student's mother, someone I had admired, said to me, "You let him do that?" For a few seconds, a rush of embarrassed guilt washed over me. Something in my son's behavior that had made me smile was being judged harshly. It took me a couple of private seconds before I realized that her obnoxious comment was designed to inflict the pain of guilt. Zach loved his shirts and was learning his numbers. I was doing nothing wrong and certainly not something violating any code of conduct. I think I answered defending myself, but I'm not really sure.

Guilty whammies can come from anywhere and everywhere when you're a mom. We play the guilt game so well, don't we? Yet it is such a waste of time. Let *good enough* be your guide and get over guilt fast. Go past it. If need be, apologize for some legitimate faux pas and make the last best move, as my friend from Ohio was able to do here. In this Ding Dong Ditch game, both mother and son emerge as winners.

. . . .

Play His Game

He is hiding behind a garage in between garbage cans, across the street from a house where a police cruiser's lights are flashing red. There are voices on a walkie-talkie. He doesn't know his friend's whereabouts. The two are in ninth grade and it's about eleven o'clock on a Saturday night. Sweating in abject, never-before-experienced fear, he can smell the remains of someone's dinner, and it doesn't have appetizing appeal. Will they find him? What will happen then? Will he be arrested?

Should he turn himself in now? But his legs won't let him. He needs to calm down, to stop shaking. Why did they run? Well, of course they ran, stupid. That's all part of the game.

Ding Dong Ditch has been their Saturday-night staple all spring. Not everyone plays it their special way, of course. You hide a video camera in the shrubbery near a darkened front door. Position it so that it will catch the face in the open door. Turn it on. Then ring the bell, run like a nitwit, and hide nearby to catch the action. When someone comes to see who's there, the camera records the surprise. People make the funniest faces, they've learned. He and Pete are so good at this game by now that they are considering careers in cinematography, just like that guy on *Dawson's Creek*. Even better, didn't Steven Spielberg start out this way? All of their friends have been captured on the tape in the video camera tonight, but the real stars of the show—the faces from their Ding Dong Ditch expeditions—don't know where their surprised looks are landing.

Tonight, however, he and Pete have rung one doorbell too many and hit not a jackpot expression but a cesspool of trouble. A guy crazy with anger came out with a gun. He can only guess where Pete has gone in his haste to escape, but he does know that they are both in deep sh-t. Don't use that word. Your mother doesn't like it. And she's not even home until Sunday night. He's supposed to sleep over at Pete's again tonight, but he'll have to find him first. Where is Pete?

It hasn't been a good year for her. Oh, nothing horrible has happened—no cancer, no deaths, no divorces—but her husband accepted a job in Virginia, and she opted to stay put in Ohio until her daughter finished this last year of high school. The younger one, her tuba player, has had a nice freshman experience in spite of their disjointed family life. Moving everyone last September just didn't make sense. Now, after nearly nine months of flying back and forth once a month and house hunting in an area where prices just don't line up financially with their own ten-year midwestern investment on Briarwood Drive, she is frustrated and really tired. Her compassion for single mothers has also shot up to sky-high proportions. Single-parenting two teenagers hasn't been easy. Extracurricular activities alone are a killer.

At the outset, she thought it might be nice to give up the responsibility for those family dinners, but the truth is, she misses the former burden of cooking for her family of four. She and the kids have been grabbing anything on the run. Meanwhile, several states away at a Fairfield Inn, her husband jokes about eating pizza nightly in his boxers on the motel bed. Damn, if only she could find a comparable house near his new office, she would be so much more optimistic. They need to be together.

He, the fourteen-year-old, stayed with a friend this past weekend. She flies into Dayton, an hour from home, late on Sunday evening with just enough time to pick him up, throw in a load of laundry, and get ready for bed. She's tired. Wouldn't it be wonderful to be sound asleep by eleven? Actually, she's hoping for an even earlier lights out. She's got to be up by six in the morning, but there's the issue of her daughter, who has been visiting a college this weekend with two girlfriends. A student from last year's class invited them. She'll have to wait up.

She calls her freshman from the car to tell him to be ready for his pickup. She doesn't want to socialize with Pete's parents, even though they are good friends and great people; she's just tired. They will understand. He's ready and waiting at the door.

Talk in her car is minimal.

"Did you have a good time with Pete?" she asks.

"Sure," he says. "His parents are cool. They let us use the video camera again." He's thinking, Should I tell her now or later?

"That's nice," she says, totally uninterested.

Later. He'll do it later.

This most recent trip has been a disaster for her. Housing prices are out of their reach. A comparable four-bedroom with any yard at all is way over $350,000 and they are headed toward a closing in thirty days on their current home that is bringing in nowhere near that much. The last thing on her mind is her son. He's been such a good kid. Most of her parenting energy has gone into his sister's senior year push with those college applications, visitations, proms, and graduating perks. It all went so fast.

At home now, she's about to cry when the front doorbell rings. Who could that be? Her daughter has just called from the road and isn't due in for at least another forty-five minutes. Flipping on the front-porch light, she turns the brass lock, grabs the knob, and opens the door.

Her heart drops at the sight of a policeman. Mother Fear is the most amazing emotion, isn't it? Childless friends simply can't begin to understand this whiplash ride we have no choice but to take. Oh. Oh. Oh. Just like in the movies, her hand goes to her chest. Her mouth is half open and in that slice of seconds before the officer speaks, she thinks, Someone has been hurt. Her daughter? Her husband? Her sister? The only person it can't possibly be is her son. He's upstairs.

"Ma'am," he begins cordially. "We're investigating a complaint and I believe it concerns your son."

"My son?" she says, shocked. "Are you sure?"

His facts are correct. There's been no mistake. Pete, whose name she reads upside down on the officer's pad, is part of it.

"I'll get him," she says. "He's doing his homework. Would you like to come in?" Her mind is buzzing. The calm surface is so fake.

She escorts the officer into the living room and, with wobbly legs and lurching stomach, she rushes upstairs. You always hate being caught ill informed about your own kids. What the hell was he doing? Confronted in his bedroom, he is sitting at the computer but drops his head in guilty fear when she asks, "Why would a police officer be at our front door tonight?" He's never been in trouble, so she has no frame of reference for this new territory. Is this just the beginning of big trouble up ahead?

His fear is wrapped in guilty agony. "Oh God, Mom. I'm so sorry. Pete and I were just playing Ding Dong Ditch and this guy went crazy over on Bellevue Terrace. I was going to tell you but I thought it could wait until tomorrow. You were so tired and grouchy." Now she's the one feeling guilty.

"What is this Ding Dong Ditch?" she asks, but as he tries to tell her something about a movie and the video camera, she interrupts. "No, wait a minute. Let's go downstairs so you can explain it to the police officer and me both at the same time. Come on. He's sitting in the living room." When he stands up from his desk chair, his height suddenly surprises her. When did he grow so tall? Then his voice cracks. That "Aw Mom" goes from high pitch to big-boy low in a wink.

"Okay."

Downstairs, the three sort out facts. The good news is that he's not being arrested. The bad news is that he and Pete will be doing community service on their summer vacations.

Ding Dong Ditch? Let me tell you about this game. All the middle school–age kids had been playing it on warm spring evenings until it grew to a pitch of aggravating nuisance, which is why the police started to take it seriously. Calls from homeowners to headquarters had reached an investigatory point, but the poor fellow on Bellevue had a particularly hairy angle in his own predicament. A stalker had been haunting his nineteen-year-old daughter. A restraining order had even been issued to keep her from harm's way. This father, out of desperation, had purchased a gun, legally and for protection, and the boys simply met his legitimate but mistaken wrath by choosing his house. He was sick and tired and actually very frightened for his child's sake. Furious, the man had been talked out of pressing more serious charges, the police officer explained.

"How did he identify the boys?" she asks.

"The video camera was left in the bushes and when our patrolmen scoured the neighborhood, we confiscated it," he explains. "We might not have been able to track down the boys if it weren't for the film still in the camera."

"Film?" she asks.

The officer looks over at her son. "Sure, it's funny. We actually watched it at the station and when the credits rolled, their names appeared on the tape."

"What credits?" she asks.

The officer looks at her son. "Did you show your mom the movie?"

"Well . . ." he starts to explain, stops, then starts again feeling panicky. "No. You see, my dad's in Virginia and she's been really busy with my sister." His voice trails off with the realization that he is obviously offering too much information in answer to a simple question that has been boxed in complications.

The officer turns to her and smiles. "Their film is pretty good, actually. We got a kick out of it."

The video camera has been returned to Pete's parents. Both boys have received their summer marching orders and will be getting community service assignments from the social worker assigned to the juvenile division. Pete's dad, who had been furious with his son, has calmed down. On the telephone, they had been able to laugh about Ding Dong Ditch. And now, long past her dream of an early bedtime, she is sitting on the side of his bed—something she hasn't done in many months.

"So did you ever find out where Pete was hiding last night?"

"Oh sure. He was so scared about losing his dad's camera that he was under the neighbor's front porch there in Bellevue. Pewwww, did he stink. Some rabbits must live under there." They laugh. It's quiet.

Of course, she could feel guilty about having been so busy that she had disengaged from a few details in her son's life. They need to reconnect.

"Hey kiddo, want to take in a movie tomorrow night?" she asks.

He pauses and it dawns on him. "You mean my movie?"

"Definitely," she says.

The truth is . . . she's not going to feel guilty. Guilt, she is telling herself, is a waste of emotional energy and time. And time, of course, is such a precious commodity that she wants to spend it wisely.

The Art of
Learning the Truth

....

Once adolescence begins, teenage boys go to their room, close the door, turn on the stereo, and come out four years later," Anthony Wolf, Ph.D., says jokingly in his super book, *Get Out of My Life, but First Could You Drive Me and Cheryl to the Mall: A Parent's Guide to the New Teenager.* So your son may crave privacy and treat you like an untouchable. As he shuts you out with silence or hostile barbs aimed right at your heart, all that reassurance drawn from books about teenage psychology doesn't quite alleviate the hurt. It really can hurt when a boy is hateful. Forget the fact that you understand this disappearing act on an intellectual level. Yes, he's normal (or at least you hope so), and doing his boy thing. What is he doing in there anyway? Could he be masturbating? Gambling on-line? Dabbling in anything illegal? Becoming seriously depressed? Should you expose the fact that you know about the shoe box under his bed holding the porn flicks? Better not. Keep that piece of information in check for a later airing of the laundry.

Knowledge is definitely power, and if he's not going to tell you much or he feels he needs to hide the truth, you need friends and alliances, not only for commiseration or tearful exchanges, but for the kind of intelligence gathering all moms love.

Seek Secret Allies

He is fourteen years and eight months of age. He's also six feet one, 180 pounds, and has grown more than eight inches in two years. "Oh my God," she recalls, "the first time he lifted his arms and I saw all that hair in his pits, I had to call my mother. I look at him now and think, 'Oooooooo, what happened to my little boy?' He's gone and in his place is this big, this big . . ." She pauses. "Well, he's this big gangly boy who shaves and not just once every two weeks but every day now." This is her third child but the first boy. The girls, well, the girls were just different . . . not necessarily easier. His sisters love him, but they are away in college now.

Because she manages a part-time youth employment service with offices right in the high school across from the cafeteria, her ears are always tuned in to local adolescent frequency waves. She can call the security guards confidants. Just ask Wade, who's been policing the halls and courtyards for more than thirty-five years. He knows her. Yet she doesn't have a fix on this freshman class yet. This is the same public school she attended way back when. Right now, she is still clueless about who is in the fast crowd and who isn't. Then again, it's only the end of September. Give it time. Soon she'll know.

A new form of weekend entertainment has started: Someone invites a few friends over and if no parent happens to be around, another fifteen, twenty, or even one hundred teenagers show up. On your doorstep. In your front yard. Out back. On the curbs. At the corner. If no one can definitively say, "Go away or I'll call the cops," the kids either get inside using back doors or basement windows or they simply hang around outside creating havoc.

A couple of other moms she knows, all connected to a boy on the freshman high school football team, are sitting in the bleachers after a game late one Friday afternoon. Waiting for the locker room to empty out, no one goes anywhere because these boys are not the drivers in their own lives yet. "We're a pretty mixed group," she points out. Skin color is unimportant around here in local parental anxiety circles. No one is immune. Oh, maybe a geek or two. But those moms just have other kinds of worries. He is one of seven white boys on a team of thirty kids with nicknames like Moose and Lightning. They call him White Boy. "There we are, three or four black moms, and three white moms waiting, waiting, when someone asks, 'Where's your kid going tonight?' "

She has to say, "Are you kidding me? I don't know."

Soon these moms start comparing notes and concurring. "Oh, is your son wandering around town too?" The moms agree that husbands are more likely to let go and pass off the wandering with the rationale that boys will be boys, but as a group, the women all want to know, "Where is he? What's he up to?"

"Thank God I have no social life," she says. "No, seriously, my husband and I do go out occasionally, but even then, I'm the parent who waits up for our son, all the time thinking, 'All right, where is he now? He's got five minutes to get back into this house.' "

Oh, he's a good kid, though. Don't get her wrong. She sits

on his social life, letting him spread his wings but not quite far or wide enough to get hurt. "Teenagers in this generation are just so far from where we were at their age." She sighs. "So far. Even the fast kids I knew weren't into some of the things kids do now. I mean, being in the fast crowd meant that you went out behind the garage and smoked cigarettes. I wasn't in the fast crowd. I just watched from afar. We didn't watch *Sex and the City* on television. Now you never know what's going to happen. You just never know. It's called peer pressure, but I don't think that at fourteen he needs to be guzzling booze and smoking dope and all that. I hear things when I drive boys around. The absolute best way to find out what boys are doing is by volunteering to car-pool."

Up there in the driver's seat with the radio bee-bopping, she has listened to every word being spoken in the back. "Do you realize that girls were performing oral sex on some boys in a baseball dugout?" she asks me. "This blew me away. One girl would go down on a row of boys. Can you imagine? Everybody watched and it was like playing Spin the Bottle but it was oral sex for entertainment. You could have picked my chin up from the floor when I heard bits and pieces in the car and then my friend told me more about it."

She's plugged in, and she's the kind of mom who confronts her son. She waits for the comfortable moment, usually in the kitchen when he is grabbing something to eat. At snack time, she'll hit him with Twenty Questions.

"Aw Mom," he whines, rolling his eyes at her, "you know me better than that. I wouldn't have been in that dugout." But does she really know him? This is the same child who was suspended from school in eighth grade for possession of a dangerous weapon. Her son!!! Hanging out in their backyard, a group of his pals apparently uncovered an old knife in a wooded area. Someone took it home, cleaned it up, and arrived the next day to show it off. Her boy—the same kid she thinks she knows so well—put it in his locker but by lunchtime, with the metal door open, he proceeded to show it off to anyone within peeking distance. Of course, he was caught.

"This was a *big* knife," she says. "Heaven forbid. Columbine had just happened. What was he thinking?"

The incident has now disappeared without a trace of a police record. Suspended from school, grounded for a month, and embarrassed to the nth degree, he is aware that this is a weapon at her disposal. She uses it skillfully; it's a piece of artillery that comes in handy. "I remind him what can happen when he doesn't think first. If you ask me what my biggest fears are, I must say that I am afraid of his making poor judgment calls that could be dangerous to himself or somebody else."

One morning at school she picks up the scent of something stinky in a ninth-grade social circle. "Wade," she explains, "is a tremendous source. The word was out that this particular freshman class had been very busy on the weekend. Some boy even peed in an empty beer bottle and a very drunk ninth-grade girl had been dared to drink it."

She cringes reflexively. Doesn't your own mouth go dry and icky? "You can just see it, can't you?" she asks. Oh, nausea.

Was he at the party? She can't be sure. It was a typical week-end night. In fact, it was the very same night he had consumed pounds of chicken Parmesan, pasta, and cake at 6:30 at a friend's house and then wandered out for pizza uptown at 8:30. She knows, because she made the cake. "A huge dinner. I saw it. Those boys have enormous appetites. Sometimes I can't believe what they can consume," she recalls. But *no*, they couldn't just stay put or go where they said they were going to be. They had to go wandering all over town. 'We were hungry,' he told me when I caught up to him later."

Now she's worried. Did he appear to be drunk when he got

home? Think. She doesn't remember hearing upheavals or upchucking behind the bathroom door. No, he couldn't have. He wouldn't have. He's too private a kid to pee into a beer bottle for public consumption. After all, he showered with his boxers on for an entire ice hockey season when the team was required to clean up at the rink before heading off to first period. Honestly, he actually left his underwear on when he took a shower. Wet boxers. Oh, God. That must have felt terrible.

Stay focused. Set the pee-in-the-bottle story aside. It's not him. Get back to work. She's at school. Later, his astronomy teacher spots her in the hallway and asks about a permission slip that needs to be signed in order for him to go on the field trip to the planetarium. A promise to track it down puts her hand directly into his backpack later that day. She sees the note then. Not the permission slip; this note has his penmanship along with someone else's. It must have been passed back and forth in a class and it alludes to public school kids being admitted free and girls being good to go, but private school kids would have to pay to get into the party. Someone's brother was bringing a "forty." What's a "forty"? she stops to wonder. Is beer being sold in packs of forty? Does she need to research parenting adolescent boys in a liquor store? Then she's scared. This note is old, judging by the condition of the paper and its placement at the bottom of the backpack. Could he have peed in a bottle? Offered it to a girl? Watched her drink it and throw up?

Hyperventilating while waiting for him to arrive home from an away game, she never lets him sit down or start snacking when he does finally reach the kitchen.

"I've got something to talk to you about," she says.

Standing in the doorway, he's in her firing zone. "The poor kid was about to be browbeaten for sure," she recalls.

"What now?" He puts up a defense shield.

"I'm not very happy with some of the things I'm hearing at school about the freshman class."

"What things?" He gives her that look. You know the one. The angry, insulted expression that shouts, Mom, you don't know anything. This is so stupid.

"So I guess you don't know anything about the party where the girl drank the pee in the beer bottle." Stomach twisting. Heart beating. His. Hers. Of course, both of them are engaged in battle.

"And I guess you don't know that you can get very, very sick from ingesting urine," she keeps on going. "This girl is very lucky."

Nothing in return.

"So I guess you weren't there?" She listens to her own voice move up the scale.

"No, I was at Tim's house," he says. She can feel a crack in his armored door opening.

"Oh really? I called there and spoke to his mother," she says. Stop that. Don't go there. Don't let him know she actually did try to investigate his whereabouts. "I just need to know where you are in case anything comes up. I don't want to be the last person in town to know what my son has been up to. I need to stay in the loop for both of us."

"Well, I *was* at Tim's for a while. I wouldn't lie about that." To be honest, he was all over town and still home by 11:30. Amazing.

Aha. From her pocket, she pulls the note that she found in his backpack, the one with the promise of someone's brother bringing a forty and the game plan for invited guests. Uh-oh. He recognizes the wrinkled piece of paper immediately.

"Oh, Mom, that was just a joke."

Some joke. She smiles tightly. She knows that it was no joke and he knows she is on to him. Moving from anger to denial, he walks a few steps into the dining room, where he stands for a second before putting his hands up to his face. She's watching. Don't go after him. Let him come to you. This doesn't feel like an escape yet. He leans over the back of a chair now. Such a big boy. He's awkwardly uncomfortable there. Wait. Wait now. This silence is not golden, but it may offer her a gift.

Finally, without looking back at her in the kitchen, he says, "All right, Mom, do you want to know what's *really going on*? I'll tell you what's *really going on*." He's definitive. Going to give her something.

Her heart stops beating. She's thinking, Oh, no. Please, God, let what's *really going on* not be too too awful.

"Yeah, some of my friends do smoke dope and some of them do drink, but I don't. They do. And I've told them that I'm not comfortable with it. You know our coach. I don't want to get thrown off the football team, so I don't do it, but that's just the way it is and I'm not about to change it."

There. He's said something that has been bothering him. She feels better but is still not certain about what's *really going on*. Yet, she's relieved. The air is clearer. "Tears are running down my face," she recalls. "Tears are running down his face next," she remembers. On to a lesson, she tells him that peer pressure is such a difficult thing but that she is proud of him because it takes a very strong, very special person to withstand this kind of pressure. She feels better. He feels better.

"I didn't pee in the bottle, Mom," he says. "I'd never do that."

She believes him . . . at least the part about the pee.

Is it true that he stands tall and righteous in the face of all peer pressure at parties and during weekend wanderings? Maybe not, she tells her husband. Is this the end of the story? Not at all.

"This was a good conversation because we aired some dirty laundry," she says.

His father agrees. He's reading the paper. Her mind can't stop clicking, considering the next move. Yet, she's suddenly exhausted.

"It's not that the laundry is absolutely pristine clean or that it hasn't been doctored up a bit, but at least the issues are out on the table now, don't you think?"

Of course, he says, confident that she really does know best as far as this kid is concerned. For her, the truth is that she doesn't need to know the whole truth and nothing but the truth right there and then. Airing dirty laundry was all she needed. Tomorrow she'll catch Wade and fill in the missing pieces to get the rest of the story.

The Art of
Opening Closed Doors

There is a Hindu proverb that states, "They who give hold all things, they who withhold have nothing." Our boys are unassembled puzzles on occasion and by giving them part of ourselves, we help them put the pieces of their adolescent act together. Every son is different, of course. Every family has different values, and your community is different socially, geographically, and economically from my town. No one else but you knows what your son needs to grow up. For kids maturing under the weight of a divorce, the puzzle can be even trickier to assemble. Though we moms may want to remain in control of our son's development, the reality is that struggling to become an adult is complex and disorderly for some boys. You don't always have control. You just can't. Neither can he.

One thing that may be important to remember is that your son has not walked in your footsteps. He doesn't really know where you've been. Intellectually, you don't have to share all your dark mysteries. Forcing him to carry any of your burdens is pretty stupid. And it wouldn't be fair. But it's also not fair to assume he doesn't need pieces of both his parents. Follow his lead, if you can, offering enough honesty to let him understand you. And, as you'll learn from this mom's case, don't hesitate to go back and open doors (ever so delicately, holding head high, please) in order for him to work out the puzzle of his identity.

Give In

So, you think you know your son. Well, so did she. You think you understand the consequences of your actions. Well, so did she. Then, one day, you get slammed silly and have to look twice and then, again and again, at both your child and yourself.

It happened last weekend. Now, it's Monday morning. The photo sits on her desk at work, just to the left of her computer monitor. He gave her the frame for that last birthday. He's a sweetheart when he wants to be. She sighs. He's wearing gigantic painter pants and that humongous navy polo shirt with the red diamonds she purchased last Christmas. It had to be extra large, even though his frame is hardly that yet. Arms crossed in front, he's in a confident slouch. Is that a chip on his shoulder? Could be. Behind aviator glasses, he squints at the camera. His lips are sealed tight. There is no smile. It's a smirk, in fact. Why hasn't she noticed how his ears stick out a little, just like his father's? How he rarely smiles around her anymore?

He's her fifteen-year-old rapper, a freshman in a North

Carolina high school, and she's looking closely at this snapshot because she's trying to see signs of a party animal in this son's demeanor. That's how his friend Kiran described him to her last weekend on the front porch. A party animal? Her son? How could that be? And a shoplifter? The CDs and adult magazines he was caught with at the mall were what prompted her conversation with Kiran on Sunday morning. This was private girl talk. Woman to young woman, she wanted to know more about his petty theft. This news of his party-animal status arrived as a bonus bit of information that has now blown her perceptions to pieces.

She divorced his father, a minister, when he was two and his big brother was four. The mistake of her marriage was at least two years old at that point, too. This is a man who insisted on adoration and when he couldn't always get it from her, he had no trouble finding it elsewhere, even among his own parishioners. He remarried almost immediately and is now on wife number three. (She was his first.) They live within minutes of her but her path doesn't cross their orbit. She steers as far away from that hurt as she can possibly go. Ugly memories.

As for marriage again, for her, once was enough. She goes out, has men friends, but remarriage has never been her fondest wish. Not at all. It was hard enough for him and his brother to move back and forth between two households in the joint custody she agreed on. This kid was like a bounced check, she says, laughing. To add a stepfather into the stew would have been totally unnecessary. But maybe she should have. Now look what's going on. Caught shoplifting, he's also emerged as a party animal. What else doesn't she know about her youngest?

"I thought I was in control. And I had been so fair with him," she tells me. "He's fifteen and I know kids his age are going to be tempted to try lots of things, testing their wings, you know, but I thought it was just normal. Kids will be kids, after all. You've got to give them some rope, don't you think? I'm lenient, I guess. I just remember being a teenager and hating my parents for being too strict. They never let me do anything. I've let my boys push off without much punishment from me. I drink. I like parties. I like music. Why shouldn't they? But then there's this shoplifting. What's that all about?"

The call from the police came on a weekend when he was scheduled to be with his father but an out-of-town conference had forced a change of plans. He had seemed relieved on Friday afternoon when his stepmother phoned to explain. He had taken the news with a shrug. No big deal. But perhaps that wasn't the case at all, she thinks now. By Saturday morning, social seeds had been planted, and she dropped him at the shopping center to meet up with his buddies. He and his little rapper friends were cut-ups. They always made her laugh. She was happy he had friends he had held on to after eighth grade. Kiran, their next-door neighbor, who has been in his classes since first grade, has also been a lifesaver. She knows that Kiran is the only person in his life who has never made fun of him. Small for his age and so insistent on wearing those huge clothes, he leans toward the geeky end of the boy spectrum and that can be frustrating for a kid who dreams of being cool.

Yes, that's what she is seeing now. She hasn't noticed before. Now she's looking closely and she sees a lot more insecurity than she wants to admit or acknowledge.

Later, at home, after work and dinner dishes, she goes looking for him. He's glued to the computer screen and won't turn his head. She continues anyway, trying to ignore the get-away-from-me firewall he has put up.

"You know I would have given you the money for those CDs," she says. He has a court date later in the month and they've been told he will probably be compelled to do community service, maybe even at the mall. She laughs and, trying to make light of the whole issue, adds, "I don't think I would have kicked in money for those raunchy magazines, however." She's insistent on pulling some sign of emotion from him, maybe even a grin in return.

"Hey, kiddo, are you there?" she says, still trying to be pleasant.

He's not giving her anything and scowls, "Ma, you are totally too fair. Way too fair. I hate you sometimes. I do."

Be quiet. Don't cry. You are the adult. Sit down on his bed.

"Hate you. Hate you. Hate you," he says. "You are so blind."

"Oh, I am so sorry."

Then, his hate shifts in direction. "I hate myself. Hate. Hate. Hate. School is so boring. My friends suck. My life sucks. I have been drunk so many times this past year that I can't even count them. You know something . . ." He pauses, winding up for a big punch here. "You are so stupid. You don't see anything."

"Oh, but I do see," she says quietly. "I really do. It's just been so hard for me too."

"It's harder for me," he screams.

And of course, it is. She just hasn't wanted to see that until now. He storms out of his chair, glaring at her as he races off and down the stairs, leaving her with this walloping belt of anger she has never seen from him before.

So still, so very still, she stays right there on his bed while his words ring in her ears: *You don't see anything.* That's what happens, doesn't it? In order to function, to pull family life together, especially as a single mom, sometimes you do close your eyes to what you can't fix. That's survival. Don't say it. Don't see it. Maybe it will all go away. The funny thing is, sometimes it does go away. Her older son is doing just fine, thank you. Sometimes choosing to ignore and turn away from those small, festering issues isn't okay at all. Yes, she had heard him throw up in the downstairs bathroom last summer. Yes, she had debated about going downstairs to confront him. No, she thought he could handle it on his own. His brother hadn't wanted her confrontations. This is all such uncharted territory in mothering. What works for one kid is a failure with the next—even when they were born with the same genetic material.

But this is a big deal. Think clearly. Go back to the issues at hand: shoplifting. Why do people shoplift? Especially when they have money in their pockets? Why is he doing this? Why is he so angry?

A few hours later, she decides to call her sister, the mother of three boys who are now contented young adults. "I just needed to talk out his issues with someone else," she recalls.

But before she can dial that number, the phone rings. Her ex-husband is on the phone.

"He is here and very upset," she's told. "He wants us to sit down together." She is rarely in the same room with this man and has kept it that way for a decade. They communicate through the kids. All those visitations, drop-offs, and pickups were handled within shouting distance. What's more, she has believed that cutting him out of her life was the best move she ever made. It was . . . for her. And yet . . .

"Sure," she answers, suddenly seeing that her decision to distance herself so completely from her son's father was a mistake that has come back to haunt his youngest child, her confused kid. Here's that piece of his puzzle she hasn't been able to place.

"I'll be right over," she answers. "Tell him I'm on my way."

And the same kind of courage it took to walk away from marriage when this boy was only two, made her able to return . . . for his sake. The truth is, though she had never needed a man in her life, this kid did. Shoplifting and running away were signals he had sent very clearly. She realizes tonight that she is luckier than many divorced mothers. This ex-husband of hers has actually stayed close by and is willing to open the door to his son. Self-centered and a bit obnoxious in her book, the man might not be perfect. Boy, could she back that up with all the ways he had wronged her. But her job right now is to let this father into the circle of his boys' lives with a little more grace and acceptance than she's been capable of coughing up before. Oh, no, she doesn't have to love the man anymore, but both her boys have to sense that he's no longer on her condemned list. Locking her ex-husband out of her life is getting her son into trouble. And that's the last thing she wants.

The Art of Being Brave

Novelist James Carroll says, "We spend most of our time and energy in a kind of horizontal thinking. We move along the surface of things . . . but there are times we stop. We sit still. We lose ourselves in a pile of leaves or its memory. We listen and breezes from a whole other world begin to whisper."

I remember the first few months of my son Zach's life. Time became such a precious, painfully spent commodity. He didn't sleep through the night for so many months . . . was it really eleven? And we were exhausted. The only way to think was horizontally, because there was no energy available to delve beneath the surface or smell those roses everyone tried to point out. I didn't stop, sit still, or hear any whispers from any other world for a long time. Then, a hard-won comfort level and regularity helped our household to right itself. We emerged from the time-warped cocoon of early parenting to realize that there was certainly going to be a cognitive life afterward. The memory of this out-of-focus period was a familiar road map when Maggie was born several years later.

Sticking to a horizontal path, as I did after both of my children's births, is all we can do in certain circumstances. You just have to postpone thinking clearly or seeing straight when you need to avoid something painful, scary, or just plain out of the everyday norm, don't you? Deciding not to decide anything is every mother's right. Yet, I think a sign of real bravery is opening your eyes to the truths being whispered (or shouted) from that other world and then acting on your instincts.

Open Your Mind

She's known for a long time. Or maybe not so very long at all. Take a deep breath. Don't feel sorry for yourself. Everything will be okay. You, of all people, should know that. You grew up always knowing something no one else wanted to know.

He's seventeen and on the tennis team. Oh, this son is so very handsome. Just like her younger brother, the kid brother who is gay. This son, a senior in high school, is her only child and they have raised him in the West. Who would have ever thought she would end up out here? Yet, she's been very happy and has never missed the East Coast buzz or that weather. He's got no big brothers or little sisters but, thanks to her husband's family nearby, he does have cousins—girl cousins who have been his playmates from day one. Thank goodness for them, she thinks now, sitting in her neat kitchen, looking out and wondering where the afternoon will take her.

Thirteen, fourteen, even fifteen years ago, her little boy, with his dark hair, hazel eyes, and easy smile, could have been a child model. People would stop her on the street to say so. She's still proud of how handsome he is. But there has always been that other concern. Every day, even after nursery school and long into his grammar and middle school years, he would play house, Barbies, and beauty shop with Britney, Brooke, and Lauren. Eventually, when those messages about acceptable boy behavior and what it meant to be masculine in America began to sink in, her son would pretend that his three cousins were forcing him to play. She knew better. He loved making Barbie look glamorous for her date with Ken. Little-girl games made him so very happy. You just know your own child, don't you? You know when he is happy and when he is miserable.

Lately he's been miserable. When was it that she knew that he knew he was not like other little boys? She tries to reach back and pick out occasions that typified her child—the Barbie fascination? The dress-up games? Shying away from boys his own age? Frilly Halloween outfits before he knew better? Her husband would wonder, "Why doesn't he have any friends his own age? I mean boys," he'd add, not intending to throw blame or stereotype his own child but noticing that the girls were in the playroom once again and Barbie's purple and pink motor coach was parked by the door.

We talk by telephone but more often by e-mail. This isn't easy at all, even in our current culture of homosexual acceptance. My God, even the TV sitcoms have pulled gay men from the closet, haven't they? Yet, walking that straight line of American masculinity would be so much easier all around for everyone, wouldn't it? Her husband is certainly a guy's guy. Why couldn't her son take after his father? What would have been so wrong about that? Oh jeez. Stop right there. Don't go in that direction. Her boy is a remarkable, intelligent, lovely human being and she loves him soooo very much. Let go of all those what-ifs. He'll be out in the world too soon and on his own away in college.

Imagine his adolescence, or any boy's, for that matter. Nature does such cruel things to boy bodies. It makes them grow in odd proportions, cracks voices, oils faces, and puts hair in places no sane person would want. Oh, she admits begrudgingly, some boys do appear to take adolescence in stride: football players who win academic scholarships and manage to charm the entire adult world while never suffering the humiliation of acne, let alone the sense of being an outcast. Her son, is he an outcast? She's not sure. She just suspects. His pain stood out so prominently in middle school. She'd ignored it. Did everyone else see too?

"Is there something wrong with me?" he'd ask.

"Of course not," she'd reassure him.

Nothing she said helped change his mind, even daily choruses of "Oh, but you are just perfect" and "You'll like yourself more when you are older." She couldn't win and just had to keep on talking but not about everything on her mind, of course. Some things were left unsaid.

Year after year, they would sign him up for soccer. Her husband coached for a couple of years. It was a painful experience for everyone, and even worse after his father stopped coaching. He would return from those games and practices and race to his room, screaming, "I want to kill myself." Calming down by tenth grade, he gave up soccer, discovered tennis, and became determined to do everything he could to fit in . . . being named a team captain, taking his pretty cousin Brooke to a Christmas dance, sending secret valentines to that girl in earth history class. All along, she could see that he was in a world of his own, even among his peers. There was no one he knew who was quite like him. That was it: he had no real peers.

"As a mom, you know what you see, but in this case, I tried

not to look too hard. I didn't want to see him for who he was. I thought maybe he'd outgrow a phase or that puberty would change him into that all-American masculine guy and that his leanings as a little boy were just a little-boy thing. The Barbie phase had to pass, didn't it? But how could I think that? I was the adult. I was the big sister who knew even more clearly than most people in the world what it meant to grow up gay and not have anyone recognize it. He didn't know why he didn't like kissing the girls at those teenage parties. He couldn't understand why he found it so hard to be like the other boys or why he preferred talking to his female cousins about boyfriends, hairstyles, and clothes. I should have been more proactive. I know it."

Last weekend was Thanksgiving and her brother brought a friend to the family meal served at her house this time. She loves big family parties, but this was the first time in years that everyone from her side of the clan agreed to fly west. Did I mention that her mom and dad are still in the Washington, D.C., area? Obvious to everyone—and dinner was being served to thirteen, including her great-aunt May—was the fact that this friend of her brother's was no ordinary acquaintance. This was his partner, his lover, if you dare. Oh, the two men weren't shocking or overtly romantic in their behavior. No one was uncomfortable and, in fact, they were both fun to have around. She had also forgotten what a big help her brother could be in the kitchen. No gravy from a can for him. His sauce was superb. And the stuffing would not be Pepperidge Farm. From the moment they arrived at the airport from New Orleans, it was just apparent that the two men were a couple. What was also obvious is that her son had never noticed this fact of life about his uncle.

Like someone wandering around in a dark Victorian house, her son, this big, beautiful, lost boy, was given a light switch to turn on that Thanksgiving weekend. His uncle offered him a view of another world. You could see it in his eyes and later in his efforts to stick close to his uncle and friend. Why hadn't she thought of this before? This was not something he had to deal with on his own.

"So I called my brother and asked, 'How'd you like to have some company over the Christmas holidays?' " she explains to me. She continues, "Of course, he said yes. Honestly, he loves to have family visit him in Louisiana, and we just don't go often enough. He's a big nut for Christmas decorations. Puts a tree up in almost every room. He had already started his decorating before they flew up to my house for Thanksgiving, in fact."

When she explained that it would be his nephew who would be coming on his own and that he would fly down on December 26 to spend part of his holiday break from school, her brother admitted, "I always thought he was gay."

"You did?" she asks, honestly surprised. "Why didn't you say something?"

"Well, I didn't think that was really appropriate," he answers.

"No, you're right. It guess it wouldn't have been," she says. "But I think he needs you now. I think he needs to know that he's not so alone and that there are other wonderful men in the world just like him."

"Awww, I do love you," he says.

She starts to cry a little, remembering that her brother was once her best friend in the world. Yes, he was never too busy to play Barbies with her and he would let her dress him up in the wildest outfits.

"Have you talked to him yet?" he asks.

"No, I thought I'd check with you first, but I know he'll be really excited."

That same afternoon, when her son arrives home from school, she's still at her desk in the kitchen, making holiday plans. The cookbooks are out. The computer is on. And the confirmation of an airline ticket purchase is there in her e-mail inbox. She got a good deal.

"Hi, Mom," he says. "How was your day?" His voice is lighter than it has been in months.

"Great, just great. Wait till you see what I bought you!" she says, smiling. "I could kick myself for not thinking of this sooner."

He's curious, but years of containing his emotions make him cautious.

"Check this out," she says, opening the window to the Web site so he can see his ticket order on-line.

"Mom," he says after a few minutes, looking very carefully at her expression for signs of understanding and acceptance.

"It's okay," she says. "I know. I know. So does your uncle, of course."

He puts his arms around her shoulders because they both need a hug. "I'm so sorry," she says. "I'm just so sorry I didn't think of him sooner."

"I'm sorry, too."

"Don't you ever be sorry for being yourself," she says.

"Oh, Mom, this is just perfect," he announces, looking back at the computer screen and his getaway gift.

And she realizes that it *is* the perfect time.

"Hey, not to change the subject of Christmas, but I cut this out from the newspaper for you today," she says, handing him an article about Drew University in Madison, New Jersey, one of the universities now proclaiming openly to be the right place for gay students in search of a great college experience.

"Wow. I should add this to my list," he says.

The truth is, though she would have liked to protect him

from those failures in his attempts to fit in and find himself in the heterosexual world, this was not ever in her power. She couldn't score his soccer goals, force the other kids to accept him, or take his SATs. You can't do any of it when you are a mom. Searching for his sexual identity was just as much up to him as any other milestone in his seventeen-year journey. And even though she'll keep on trying, deep down she knows that no one else can make you happy but yourself.

The Art of Blaming Genes

"Heredity isn't destiny," Dan Kindlon and Michael Thompson write in their book *Raising Cain*, but it does help us to explain a son's behavior on occasion, doesn't it? Seriously, this genetic link between behavior and biology has come ever closer to being deciphered on a molecular level. Scientists working in molecular biology and our human genome tell me that 99.9 percent of all our biochemical codes are alike. What makes us so dissimilar—more or less likely to look and act differently—is that .1 percent and the way our genes are sequenced, or spelled out, as well as our experiences. Some of the researchers I've interviewed for health stories are peering intimately in their laboratories at the miniscule molecules responsible for everything from our hair color to our odds of getting cancer. Using sophisticated tools, they are excited by what they see and how much more they understand.

This mom was pretty excited, too, when she identified frustrating behavior that had crossed the generations among the men in her life. It sure wasn't gene expression microarray analysis, as researchers might use, but her tools of observation for making the genetic connection were worth applauding. Better than any how-to parenting book with prescriptions for raising happy-go-lucky, well-adjusted teens, our own family trees can help us clear up the kind of human behavior that defies easy explanation.

Like Father, Like Son

He is seventeen and a senior in a Virginia high school not far from the beach. Don't focus on that geographic spot, however. No matter where you live, if you are the mother of a teenage boy, you know intimately how far that fascination of a kid with his car can go. We worry about accidents, crazy drivers, and what the exhilaration of having his own wheels will do to even the sanest, steadiest child. And we try to insulate our boys from all sorts of danger at the very time in their lives when we need to let them go, at least a little. You just can't keep them home, can you? They need to fly free in order to grow up. Who among us really wants to claim fame as a hovering, controlling mother? Not me. Not you. Yes, this business of separation is not an easy task at all. Sometimes the power of a boy's creative reach takes a shape we just can't anticipate and one that is all too familiar.

Yes, this boy is creative, and thrifty, too. His sense of timing? Well, that's another matter altogether. I've known her for years. They have three sons close in age, which means a triple whammy of "oh boy" adventures in child raising. What's more, her husband falls into that category of fun-loving grown-up, so she's far outnumbered in a household of daily testosterone-driven demands. She tries hard to ignore it, but we all know it's not easy to remain calm when the mess of life with men piles up, the garbage doesn't go out on time, the shoes are always in the middle of the floor, and the kitchen isn't ever picked up the way we want it to be. She can empty the dishwasher, wipe down the counters, put uneaten food into plastic bags and containers, smile when she turns off the light to go to bed, and then be aghast with the early-morning vision of what a midnight eating fest has wrought on her kitchen.

"I woke up the other morning about three A.M. to the smell of peppers and onions frying." She sighs. "They are always so hungry." Five A.M. and midnight ice hockey schedules also wreak havoc on any attempt to bring order or a sensible pattern to the household.

"My attitude toward the boys has been pretty laid-back," she says, "though I'm not sure they would agree. They have all been so good that I have little room to complain. They are great about letting me know where they are and when they'll be home. They do well in school and sports and most of their friends seem to be acceptable human beings. We pretty much do a give-and-take on issues that make me anxious. Thank God for cell phones and for eight hundred numbers. Long before they each had a cell phone, I had an eight hundred number so they never had an excuse not to call me from anywhere, anytime."

The insurance company suggests that the safest bet on the road for teenagers is a station wagon or van, so unofficial ownership of the old family Taurus wagon falls to this middle child, the seventeen-year-old senior. Right away, he gains a new crop of carless friends, all in need of rides to the beach or the mall as this blue Ford wagon with the red interior takes on new significance in more than just functional ways. He installs a $600 stereo system and a custom air filter for more horsepower. She raises her eyes. Not her voice. Clever kid. Who would have thought? She was happy to trade up for a new means of transportation, never imagining how far his creative powers would be able to take him.

"Soon the girls are calling more often, too," she says. Semi-independent financially, he works hard at a local restaurant as the banquet manager and manages his money so well that he's dabbling successfully in the stock market. Need advice or a hot tip?

A penny-pincher, he doesn't like to waste money and always shops around for sales. "Target is his favorite store." She chuckles. "Honestly, he is smart catching bargains on expensive ice hockey equipment, and you should see how well he does with sneaker purchases—though he seems to need a new pair every other day."

And yet, he spends his money on items she considers extraneous and strange. Probably because he's seventeen.

There's something unsettling here. You can see it in her expression. "He doesn't always think clearly. He's just not level-headed yet." In fact, as we muse through this car episode together, it becomes clear that he thinks more like his father, the man she loves but could sometimes almost kill on occasion.

Two stories. Two different male creative avenues with the potential to run amok. Two guys in her life.

By hearing her husband's story first, you may be better able to understand the emotional undertow of the recent scene in her driveway. She's looking back a few years now. "I was shocked and furious when I opened our front door late on a Saturday afternoon. I mean, it was really late, with just one hour of daylight left. My husband started out with the intention of replacing a few rotten boards on the front porch of our

Sunset Avenue house. Then he told me that the smell of new wood and the sound of a hammer and nails inspired him to rip the whole thing out, right down to the door frame. He was going to rebuild the entire porch, complete with bench seating and new railings. To make it exciting, he decided to use 1920s hand tools, nothing electric, no screws or power nails, no poured concrete, and he even went for the old-fashioned nails. He wanted it to look just like the old houses in Maine, and the idea had been propelled by our neighbor's enthusiasm there in the front yard. Both of them were drinking beer." They had stopped at the liquor store on their way back from the lumberyard.

She gasps, tries to hide her fury, but just can't do it. "I blew up."

There were no front steps at all, just a void that she knew from experience might stay that way for days or weeks as his efforts were sidetracked in favor of watching a football game or going to work.

Looking into her near future, she could see her pretty house remaining unrenovated for some time to come. It would look like a friendly person with no front teeth.

"The two men were admiring their demolition," she says. "I was really furious and said, 'Don't think you are coming into this house until you finish rebuilding the porch and stairs.'" She slammed the door, thought about locking it, and sat down to cry. Don't give in. Hold on to this line. There would be no wavering for her, because if she did, she knew there would be no front porch.

Trips to the hardware store for lights, equipment, and a stop for more beer inched the project along into the dark of the evening and beyond. Another neighbor joined the construction crew, and this guy actually had some experience because he was a retired builder. Lucky for her husband. She could hear them until 3 A.M., when he opened the front door and slipped into bed. She pretended to be asleep and didn't even take a peek out front until the next morning. There were steps and a deck. Thank goodness. It took two more months for the built-in benches to be completed and even more time for a new coat of paint.

On to her son. She arrives home from work to discover the entire interior of the Taurus wagon lying all over the driveway in pieces. Her son had become bored with the red interior and was going for a smooth black satin finish for the inside of the car. Cans of spray paint stood ready. There was her Taurus—yes, it's still in her name—dismantled, exactly like the car in *The French Connection.* There's about an hour of daylight left. Not enough time, her mind flashes. This is a disaster in waiting.

"What are you doing?" she asks, with a pretty good idea of exactly what he is doing. Why do we ask the obvious? Why aren't their answers always logical? Why can't we think like they do? Because, obviously, they aren't always thinking.

"I'm saving money," he says.

"Saving money?"

"Well, yeah, *Mom.*" He puts the accent on *stupid.*

"How so?" she asks, trying to stay calm but thinking back to her missing front porch in the past.

"Well, this would have cost a fortune if I had it done by a professional car detailer."

"It would?"

"Sure."

Pause. Pause. Control your temper. Go slow. You can be the logical one here. She says, "It's late and the weatherman just said it was going to rain tonight." She has a finely tuned sense of timing—unlike at least two of the men in her life, who are quite comfortable coexisting with their works in progress. If it weren't for her, nothing would ever get put back together. Humfph.

News flash: their garage is packed. What about all those car parts?

"What do you mean?" he asks. "About the weather?" he adds, honestly puzzled.

"I mean, how are you going to get it all back together before dark? You don't have enough time."

"Don't worry, Mom."

"I just do," she says, "worry. I think it's a mother's nature."

"Awww, jeez. Don't you trust me?"

She sighs. "I guess I have to, don't I?" This is not your front porch, she says to herself. Go inside. Save yourself anxiety. Don't look. This boy is just like his father.

Eventually, the car pieces fit back together, but not that day. He figures it out and finds a tarp for weather protection. Sigh. She can see that what he lacks in common sense and timing, he'll make up in ingenuity, like his dad. A week or so later, he tells her that he has picked up rims and tires on sale at Target. That makes her smile. He'll never go bankrupt, she thinks. Her Taurus no longer belongs to her and neither do pieces of this boy—clearly, those lean more to her husband.

The truth is, she loves her husband very much. He's always been the guy for her. Funny and fun-loving, even though he rarely completes projects within a time frame she finds applaudable. But who cares? Is that really important? Not at all. In the meantime, thinking about this seventeen-year-old reincarnation makes her sigh in pleasure at what Mother Nature *(errr, biology)* is capable of.

The Art of
Stopping Resentment

....

I can feel a bout of resentment coming on like the beginnings of a bad cold. I've learned to head to T. J. Maxx, a favorite shopping haunt, as soon as possible for my cure. I don't even need to buy anything to escape from seething resentment over picking up way too many wet towels, putting new toilet paper on the rolls in all three of my bathrooms over and over again, realizing that not one other person in the world knows how often I empty and reload the dishwasher or deal with the endless round of other household chores that fall naturally into every mom's domain.

Resentment, I was taught, can be a mother's downfall, and you ought to recognize it early and find your personal purge for this ugly emotion. It's easy to feel you are being taken advantage of. Families do depend heavily on moms like you. And it's nice to be needed, but an overload of work, without ever having time off for good behavior, builds resentment easily. We've all experienced resentment or we wouldn't be human. You think no one in your household understands or appreciates you. (Clench your teeth, complain loudly, or do a little seething silently here.) You believe that everybody else has a better life. You become a martyr. (Now say, Poor me. Why can't I ever...) Look closely: Have you seen resentment lately and how it poisons your atmosphere? Can you hear it in your martyr voice, even when you are trying to sound nice? This negative emotion permeates the atmosphere like toxic dust from a weapon of mass destruction.

The paths resentment takes aren't all the same, but the costs are always high. It has a voracious appetite, eating up all your fun and happy times, and it can consume you and blind you to reality. I had a wise friend who explained that resentment grows wild when you don't take time off, don't ask for help, and assume that people know what you are thinking. They don't know what's in your mind. So don't assume that they do. Speak up. The mother in this story had resented a lot about her life, even the order of her birth in a big family. She learned the hard way that it was hurting her son.

Recognize Toxic Emotions

He was her middle child, and for everyone else in the world, he wore a big smile and could do no wrong. With his high-water pants, blond hair, skinny frame (until about fourteen), and big front teeth that really could have benefited from some braces, he could charm anyone into thinking that there were nothing but angelic adventures up his sleeve. Except her. She knew better. He drove her crazy at home, pushing, pulling, insisting, nudging her into yeses when she had promised herself she'd say no. Smart, he always tested at the top of the percentiles on all the standardized examinations from first grade on. But his grades rarely reflected this intellectual capacity. Meanwhile, she was too busy with her other two children and the business of growing up herself. His older brother had been born when she was sixteen and still in high school, and he came three years later when she was nineteen and still married. His little sister followed shortly after, as well as the angry separation and ultimately amicable divorce. But her ex-husband wasn't around much. He had moved back to Florida.

He's fourteen and in ninth grade in this episode. They live about ten blocks from her parents' home in western Pennsylvania, and that makes her feel a little more secure about all the latchkey years for her kids. Past a certain age, after-school care for children is pretty much impossible. Even if she could afford the cost for all three on her paycheck, her boys rebelled long ago about being stuck in a school cafeteria from three to six every weekday afternoon. They were out and about, and until now, nothing had made her believe that this decision wasn't okay. Besides, her parents were usually home, and the kids had free rein of that household, having grown up comfortably at ease over at Gram and Pop Pop's. So she wasn't really surprised by how much time he started spending in his grandparents' basement. A new pool table, the kind with the real felt corner pockets and good sticks and cues, also made the regular pilgrimage understandable. He and his friends were polishing up their skills. Why wouldn't they want to go there every day?

Besides, his current mellow mood in the evenings was so much more bearable than the nastiness he had inflicted on her the year before. He was relaxed at dinner and had stopped torturing his little sister. In his room later, with the door closed, she even imagined him doing his homework. Something had changed for the better and she was actually hoping to see it reflected in his first-period report card when it arrived in mid-November.

To go back a little, her brother was living in Paris at the time. He and his family had been transferred there three years before and weren't expected back in the United States for another three years. Oh sure, other family members had flown over for visits, but she couldn't afford the airfare or the time off. That didn't bother her too much except at family gatherings, when talk would turn to touristy occasions and she realized what she and her kids were missing. Someday, she'd say, someday we'll go. But, in truth, any "someday" in her imagination was a long way off. Meanwhile, every time her brother or his wife came home to visit—summers, Christmas, a graduation last year—they brought another case of wine from one of their ventures into French château country. They were storing it in her parents' basement back in the laundry room, where it was cool and dark.

"Resentful?" I ask her now. "Jealous?"

"Probably. Oh maybe. Sure," she admits. "But not in any green-eyed-monster sense. I didn't want my brother's life, and mine was finally coming together after years of struggle. I was thirty-three and actually feeling pretty good about myself," she explains.

Just before Halloween, her brother arrives home in Pennsylvania on business. He's alone this time and it's a Saturday evening so everyone is invited to her mom's for dinner. She hasn't seen him since summer and is looking forward to this

friends-and-family occasion. Maybe he'll even pull out a couple of bottles of his Nuits-St-Georges *grands crus,* she remembers thinking. His last letter had described this particular wine
as if it were a beloved third child. He only has two kids, both in
private school, of course.

"He was so *into* his wine," she says. "The rest of us couldn't
imagine spending the kind of money on something that could
go down so fast. But hey, that was who he was. I guess I didn't
begrudge him. We all have our vices."

At her parents', the din of conversation is deafening, as
usual, with few listeners, only talkers among the seven siblings.
Few stop to hear in her family, to catch a drift below the surface of speech, because they are so busy jumping into the swim
of this social milieu. Newcomers can be awestruck at the cross-
chatter. Thank God there were no strangers there on that particular Saturday evening.

"At one point, my brother headed down the basement
stairs to the laundry area to bring up some of the red wine that
had been stored since the vacation trip," she tells me. "A little
while later, he came back up, cradling a couple of bottles but
looking really, really strange. He wore a puzzled expression and
called my dad over to the kitchen counter as he set three bottles down."

"Dad," he says, "do you know anything about this?"

"What?"

"Well, these empty bottles."

"Empty?" my dad hollers. "How could they be empty?"

"But sure enough, all three had been drained and, as we
soon discovered, so had three whole cases of wine," she explains. "The silence, for my family, was pretty amazing. We are
just never that quiet—but no one knew what to say or what
had happened to the wine."

The kids, all cousins, had been watching a movie in the
other room, but as the adult voices quieted down, several wan-

dered into the kitchen and dining area to see what was up. She saw her middle son, noticed him looking at the bottles on the counter, and knew in a flash who was the culprit.

"Oh my God," she says. "It suddenly dawned on me why he had been so relaxed all fall and why he had been drifting off to sleep so easily every night. He and his friends had been polishing off this very expensive wine in the late afternoons while they polished their pool skills. I was so embarrassed. I didn't even say anything at first. I wasn't sure whether exposing or accusing him there in front of everybody would be the right thing to do. And, of course, there was a teeny-tiny doubt in my mind that maybe he hadn't been the one. But I knew it, really. Deep down, I knew he was capable of such a crazy caper. Thirty-six bottles of red wine! And all those empty bottles. They put the bottles back into the boxes, but why didn't they think they'd get caught?"

Her son is quiet for the rest of the evening. She waits until they arrive home across town for the confrontation.

"I know you did it," she says angrily, not giving him a chance to deny that he and his friends drank all the wine. Why does this have to happen to her?

"I am really scared. What's wrong with you?" she says, also thinking, What's wrong with me that I couldn't recognize my own son being drunk? He sits defiantly, resentfully, not answering her. She continues, "Listen, mister, I plan to call the substance abuse counselor at school about this. You've got a problem."

"I don't have a problem."

"Yes, you do," she says. "It's a big one and you also owe your uncle an explanation, an apology, and several cases of wine."

"What if I say I don't want to apologize?" he says.

"Have you thought about how you are going to pay him back?"

"No." He pauses, then says, "He owes you, Mom."

"What do you mean?" she asks.

"It's not fair. He gets to do all that neat stuff and we don't."

"Whooooaaa. Wait a minute." The level of resentment bubbling up to the surface here shouldn't surprise her, but it does. She just hasn't recognized her own quiet, long-standing resentment or realized how it could affect her children, especially this middle son. He thinks the world, especially her family, owes him three cases of wine. He's not even acting apologetic about the theft or the underage drinking. That's pretty frightening for a mother. How could this be?

They sit for a little in silence. "Life just isn't fair, honey," she says. "But it's been pretty good to us lately, don't you think?"

"Well, I don't know," he says. A door to his anger opens a crack. "Why can't we go to Paris? Why can't you buy wine in a bottle?" She usually picks up a box at the liquor store. "They have so much more than we do. We deserve it."

"Is that what you think?"

"Well, yeah, I do," he answers.

"Really?" she asks, truly surprised at his resentment and wondering how to stop it. After a moment, she adds, "You know, your uncle has invited us to visit him in Paris more than once." Resentful of her brother's success and afraid to ask for help in paying for the trip, she had spurned the offers, and never mentioned them. That was a mistake, she can see. All the other cousins have gone across the Atlantic for a family adventure. Her mind is racing.

"How could you drink all that wine?" she asks.

"Oh, a little bit at a time," he says, "We were just fooling around at first, playing pool there in the basement. We didn't think anyone would miss it."

"Oh jeez, you can be so stupid. You know, you are never going to be able to develop a taste for boxed wine now either. Those bottles retail for more than forty dollars each, even if you can find them here in Pennsylvania. You amaze me. *Grand cru?* Do you know what that means?"

"Nah."

" 'Great growth.' "

"Ah, Mom, I'm sorry."

"Don't tell me. Tell your uncle."

"Okay. I will."

And she knew he would. The truth is . . . she's really more frustrated with him than angry now. She's also thinking about herself. Her siblings love her. She's not less good or better than any of them. She is one of them. So, she will force her son to apologize because the river of resentment in her family has grown just a bit too wide to withstand keeping this theft a secret. She herself has to stop feeling indignant about family inequities if her son is ever going to grow up happy.

"Want to go to Paris next year?"

"Are you kidding?" he asks.

"Not at all."

The Art of Communication

Word has it that one of the all-time great question askers was Henry Luce, co-founder and editor-in-chief of *Time* magazine for forty years. "Asking questions is an art," according to Jeffrey Mayer, author of *Time Management for Dummies*. You know how difficult this is to do, especially when you are too busy, as usual, or when you are being confronted with teenage escape artistry. But communicating with kids is like staying in shape for a sport. You are not going to be able to play tennis well if you haven't practiced in a long time. Keep on practicing, even when his back is turned, his eyes are averted, and his body language tries to turn you off completely.

Other tips I've picked up along the way: Face your boy when you speak. Square your shoulders with his, if at all possible. Tone of voice is critical. Consider how the word *What* can be made to sound like a curse. Upset? Wait before you tackle a topic with him. You need to be in good shape mentally before some confrontations, don't you? One expert I once interviewed for a story about teenage suicide, which was published in the now defunct *McCall's* magazine, shared this extremely wise insight: Starting a conversation with the word *Why* will always put someone on the defensive. He also pointed out that seven sentences in a row is tantamount to a lecture. Don't go there.

Hear What He's Not Saying

He and his friends have been playing on the rocks in the rear of the yard every afternoon for weeks this fall. The boys, all about twelve, have constructed a fort and seem to want to escape there all the time to pursue some sort of new game. This isn't Dungeons and Dragons. It's not the Magic cards that have captivated her neighbor's son. She is not sure what exactly they are doing, but she's happy that her son and his friends have found a way to occupy their time.

She starts to get a little nervous when they jump anxiously at the sight of her, standing outside the door to their architectural monstrosity. She's bringing snacks and juice boxes. They never even stopped in the kitchen for after-school snacks today, preferring to run straight to their fort.

"Mom!" her son shouts. "What are you doing?"

"Aren't you guys hungry?" she asks innocently. Red faces and strange looks answer her question. How weird.

On the weekend, when his older brother is off on a Boy Scout camping trip and her husband is working overtime, she decides to take him to a Sunday matinee in the city. In the car, he's feeling comfortable and relaxed, for a change. He's with his "mommy," a position she has regretfully and nearly outgrown except when they are alone on occasion. Then a question is thrown from left field, far far left field. It's a fly ball and she struggles to catch it.

"Mom, why do some women take all their clothes off for pictures?"

Look at him. Turn slowly. Don't act too shocked. What is he really asking? "Well, hon, what kind of women do you mean?" she asks casually.

"Oh, nothing. No women. Forget it," he says, backing off quickly.

"Have you seen pictures of naked women? You know, in magazines?" she asks.

"Nah. That's not what I mean."

"I know you guys have been talking about sex in school during health class. Did you see some pictures that upset you?" Ooops. She shouldn't have said "upset." He was trying to be cool.

"Can we *not* talk about this?" he says, agitated.

"No problem. Sure," she says, "but you know your dad and I are always willing to talk about anything." Almost in the parking lot now, she can let it drop too.

Later, she wonders where his inquiry came from. Her husband has talked to him about the birds and the bees. That was last year. The eighth-grade teacher recently spent a week of health classes on the subject of sex.

At home that night in bed, she turns to her mate. "Promise me you will check out their fort in the yard tomorrow," she says. "When the boys aren't around," she adds.

"What for?" he asks. "What am I looking for?"

"I don't know exactly, but I have a hunch that these boys are playing with something they don't really understand." She describes the exchange about the naked ladies.

Under rocks inside the fort, her husband uncovers small plastic bags filled with really raunchy pornographic images of women posed in some of the strangest contortions. No wonder this kid was puzzled. These are not merely naked female images. Slowly, quietly, sitting together at their kitchen table after the boys are in bed, they stare at each photo in the pack. She's uncomfortable, frightened, and then angry. There are even shots of women having sexual intercourse with animals. No wonder the boys acted so strange when she dropped in un-announced that afternoon.

When they call his best friend's mother to discuss their findings, this woman isn't surprised at all, because she had come across similar photos in a basement playroom, never dreaming they might belong to her twelve-year-old. She as-sumed his older brother had picked them up somewhere in Chicago. More calls are made and word spreads through a group of moms who are all soon familiar with the porno-graphic pictures in little zip-lock bags.

They meet. Six women . . . Six little packets of porn . . . Six nice medium-size boys discovering a seamier side of sex too soon. What are the other common denominators among them? All of the kids are in the same eighth-grade classroom. She has confronted her boy and guesses the other moms have too. What they want to know is: where did the porn packets come from?

The mothers decide on a plan of action that puts them all in the office of the new middle school principal, whose open-door policy impressed them on Back to School Night. Some have confronted their own boys. Others haven't, but what they do know is that Mr. B. is a good guy, and his last post was at an inner-city high school. This step into a suburban middle school is something his doctor recommended. You can sense that he's seen everything. He'll get to the bottom of it all.

In the office, he reassures them that sexual curiosity in boys this age is quite normal. There's nothing to worry about and he'll find out if the kids got the pictures from someone in school.

"Wait until you see them," one mom warns him as she puts a plain brown paper bag on his big desk. The photos, all of them collected and still encased in plastic, are in the bag. "Don't open it until we are gone," she says.

He laughs.

"No, seriously," she insists.

"I think I can handle it," he replies. When they are gone and he opens the bag, even he drops his jaw and raises his eyebrows. On a hunch, he heads down the hall to an eighth-grade classroom.

"So you never told me where you got the pictures of the naked ladies," she says to her son after school that day.

"What happened to them?" he asks her.

"I gave them to your principal, Mr. B., today," she says.

"Oh wow. What did he think?"

"I don't know. We didn't stick around to watch his expression when he saw the images," she says.

"Well, I didn't spend any money on them, Mom." This is a peace offering.

"Who said anything about money?" she asks.

"All the other guys had to fork over ten dollars apiece for their packets. Mine were free."

"Who gave them to you?"

"Kyle's big brother. He likes me so he didn't make me pay," he tells her.

Uh-oh. Is *that* something she should worry about now?

"Is he going to get in trouble?" he asks.

"Do you think he should?"

Her son is quiet for a few moments. "I guess so." More

silence. She's using hers wisely, in fact. "Mom, I didn't really like them very much," he says.

"That's good," she answers. "From what I saw, they were pretty scary."

"Yeah. Kind of scary. But we couldn't stop looking at them," he admits.

"I'll bet you couldn't," she says, laughing a little, putting the palm of her hand on the side of his head. "You know, real sex isn't scary. I think you'll like it when you get there, but not right now."

The truth is, she's thinking that sometimes raising boys is a little scary, too, but not right now. To be honest, these are the moments in mothering that compensate for the anguish.

The Art of Cursing

....

I love language, even in raw, or occasionally raunchy dress. What else is the speaker saying? Why the need to shock listeners? And what's behind the explosion of F---k and all its literal cousins? I work as a writing coach at Montclair High School in New Jersey, and just try walking the hallways of this public high school with ears cocked when no teachers or administrators are within listening distance. You are likely to hear the F word so often, you might assume it was a common adjective, appropriate in describing any situation, happy, sad, angry, or loving. Turn on a hip-hop or rap radio station and the language is just as loaded with meaning and I don't mean all sex and power. Something else is happening.

Michael Gurian, author of *Boys and Girls Learn Differently!*, says that most men aren't word users. Oh, there may be a few in any group who are dominant, attention-seeking males skilled in language arts, but on average, females produce more words than males.

Though girls may be adding to this chorus of curses, I can hear the F word dropping out of the mouths of boys more often. Here's the interesting part in Gurian's research, which leads me into this art of cursing. "Boys often find jargon and coded language. . . . Whether it's language from sports trivia, the law, or the military, boys tend to work out codes among themselves and within their own cognating process, and rely on coded language to communicate."

Match Code for Code

He is almost twenty and a marine, having joined after a year of college and a stab at acting school. In his recent call home, he complains about his fellow marines, and she can't help but smile. Funny, how you never can predict the circuitous path your very personal approach to mothering will take, nor the effect on your boy. Look back to where this story started: she was the second in a line of five siblings; her older brother was just eighteen months ahead. This guy loved to swear and as a teenager in his own teenage tough-guy act, f---k was the favorite word. Her brother used this expletive liberally as long as their parents weren't around to hear. He and his buddies couldn't complete a sentence without cursing. Even as a young girl, this talk would disgust her. She thought her brother and his pals' ugly language made them sound foolish and illiterate. She vowed that when she grew up and became a mother, her children would never swear.

When her son was five, he asked her what F, U, C, and K spelled. "We were alone in the car on our way home from his first day of kindergarten and I decided to keep the conversation matter-of-fact," she recalls. "Keep it simple. Don't show fear." She tells him that the letters spell *fuck* and it is a slang word for sex and making babies. He says that he saw it on a Dumpster and all the kids pointed and laughed. He pointed and laughed, too. "I told him most of those kids didn't know what the word meant either and they were probably asking their mothers or fathers about it, too." I imagined his classmates with soap in their mouths, she admits. She told her little boy that this was not a good word to use because a lot of people were offended by these kinds of slang words. Feeling oh so virtuous, she adds, "Never use this word in public, and your grandparents are definitely public."

They laugh. He's only five but he's so smart. And she feels so smart too. What a parent. This had been an open discussion. Problem solved. Her child will never swear.

Now, she's not sure when the knock-down, drag-out, win-at-all-cost swearing contests started, but they were definitely in the car alone and it was years after the smug five-year-old lesson. She may have been scolding him for something and under his breath, he called her a bitch.

"Can you imagine?" she asks. "A bitch?!!"

Quickly, she returns his "bitch" with "bastard." He's amazed. He retorts with "slut." "I called him a dickhead and he called me an asshole. I called him a prick. . . . We kept it up, rapid-fire insults, using any dirty word that came to us." She couldn't believe where all this gutter language came from. They were both shocked. Yet, a funny thing happened during their verbal dueling. Like a balloon's air being let out, the anger escaped into smirks and peals of laughter. "We were just hysterical," she recalls. "He couldn't believe that his mother knew these words. My brother had taught me well, though I hated to admit it."

Once was not enough. "Our contest rules developed over time and were understood by both of us intuitively," she says. "He who hesitated lost the game—and, yes, it was a game we played. You could not repeat a curse word," she explains now. "The game could start anytime we were in the car together, alone. The battles would break into laughter, always, always."

On this even playing field, with grown woman and young man, a cursing vocabulary grew impressively, along with other communication wisdom.

"Okay, so he swears," she'd tell herself guiltily, "but only under controlled circumstances." Yeah, right.

They never agreed to keep the contest a secret, but for years, neither spoke of it to outsiders. "It was just a game we played in the car," she says. "Once I discussed it with a co-worker, a psychologist, who thought it was just harmless fun. He said that his nine-year-old had a swearing rug in their kitchen. They had agreed she could say anything as long as she was standing on the rug."

Often, especially as he traveled through teenage territory, swearing contests were the icebreakers for serious conversations. Talk was where they went and their give-and-take exchanges were conducted on equal footing. "We discussed organized religion, sex, masturbation, abortion, marriage, divorce, homosexuality, movies, books, theater, cooking . . . no subject was off limits for us."

He is now an articulate, sensitive, open-minded young man, according to her expert calculations. She's probably right. In that phone call home the other day, he says that he can't believe how much marines curse.

"Every other crazy word is *fuck*," he complained. "They can't put a sentence together without swearing. Such foul mouths! You wouldn't believe it, Mom."

She wouldn't? Oh really. Foul language? Well, the two of them could write a book about that. The truth is, though she used to be embarrassed about their cursing game with its contest rules, she isn't anymore. Remembering those cursing battles makes her laugh out loud.

The Art of
Loving Like a Rock

On the way to work yesterday, I heard Paul Simon on the radio singing his classic "Loves Me Like a Rock," written and produced in 1973. There, I suddenly thought, is the perfect way to introduce you to this story about a son's puppy love and a mother's letting go. "When I was a little boy . . . My momma loves me . . . loves me like a rock," he nearly shouts. Isn't that the way our love goes sometimes? His lyrics are amazingly simple but so on target for where our hearts lie.

When your son starts to show signs of loving another woman, the shock can be eye-opening. Yes, it's fun to watch him begin to maneuver romantically, but his behavior can create a rather uncomfortable sensation in your gut. You may not even want to admit the emotion, because who would have ever predicted that you could be jealous of a teenage girl? Actress Debra Winger was once interviewed about her role as the mother of three boys and admitted, "Life gets trickier as you get older; it just does.... When my first child was born, director Costa-Gavras said to me, 'They break your heart every day,' and I thought, 'Oh, that is just so perfectly European and negative and I love having this baby. He fills my heart every day.' Cut to now—I've got three boys, from four to fourteen, and they break your heart every f—king day. They break it because they fill it."

Go Along with Puppy Love

He is thirteen. It's seventh grade, for heaven's sake. Let's face it, serious news about our boy's encounters with the opposite sex can snap us straight into awkward operating zones so fast. We're amazed that boys who still wear braces on their teeth, who prefer six-hour street hockey games to phone conversations with girls, who can dress for school in less than two minutes, and who still enjoy displays of parental affection would be the object of a woman's desire. Did I say *woman?* Well, I know. I know. Sorry about that. I should have said *girl* but, ahem, why does it feel like the proverbial "other woman" sometimes?

This mother is emotionally in tune and attached to all her children. This son, second in a line of four turn-around pregnancies, and her second boy, has always been talkative. Nice. We like that in a boy. Doesn't always happen, of course, but when it does, you think you have more control, more power to shape the clay from which the man will emerge. Expressive eyes, honest grin, gangly thin, he will tell her almost anything, unlike his older brother, who brushes off even casual questions with "Why do you want to know?" or the more formal "I'd rather not discuss it." Hmmmhhhfff. "Rather not discuss it" is a catch phrase she's grown to hate, in fact. Yet, both her boys are adorable and in love with her, of that she remains confident, even in the wake of this puppy-love lesson.

Her chatty child arrives home from school with big news. "I go with someone," he tells her, strutting around the kitchen like a proud rooster. Yes, a rooster. That's the word she used telling me this story.

"Really? Who?" she asks. Go with? Does this mean a girl? Wait a minute. Let him get it out. Don't push. Square your shoulders to his so he'll see your willingness to hear anything.

"I go with Kate, you know, Mom, Kate Willingham."

"Oh. The girl who used to live across the street? The one you stood next to at our bus stop?" she asks. For three years, from first to fourth grades (not so long ago), she and Kate's mother would take their kids and their coffee cups each morning to the corner. Ahhhh, little Kate, with the braids. She imagines this pretty girl now.

"The same Kate you would never speak to?" she asks, honestly reimagining the morning mayhem of rambunctious little boys with big backpacks standing alongside so many little girls. The girls, well the girls were different, even at six, and seven and eight.

"Well, I didn't know her then," he explains. Kate was on the corner with him Monday through Friday, 180 days of the year. He didn't know her? Well, now. To not know her suddenly takes on an entirely new dimension. Of course he *knew* her. He just didn't *know* her. But what is it that thirteen-year-old boys now *know* about girls that they didn't at six and seven and eight? Like one of her own children in the backseat on a long car trip, but one now being navigated by her son, she wonders, Are we there yet? Is this puberty? My God. Don't smile. Don't laugh. He must have arrived somewhere, even if it's just at the outskirts of romantic love.

"My friend Susan, you know Susan, Mom? Well, she came

up to me at lunch and asked who I would go with: Kate? Sarah? or Donna? So I thought about it and said, 'Kate.' "

He's beaming.

"Then Susan went over to Kate and asked her who she would go with: Me? Paul? or John? And she picked me." Eyebrows up, his smile is spreading.

She has to sit down at the kitchen table.

"So Susan came back to me and said that Kate would go with me if I asked her. So I walked over to Kate and asked her if she wanted to go with me and she said, 'Okay.' "

Mother and son grin, though hers is more complicated. He is so proud of himself. Should she be proud of him too?

"Do you have to carry her books now?" she asks.

"Naah."

"Do you sit with her at lunch?"

"Oh no. All the guys still sit together." Now he looks at her as if she is really out of it. What planet did she come from? How can she not know what "go with" means? Courageously, she pushes for the outside edge of this definition.

Point blank: "Well, what exactly does 'go with' mean?"

He sighs. "When we go outside, I *stand* next to her."

"Oh." Not a word, she says to herself. Don't say a word, because she could close off this precious line of communication forever if she counters with the fact that he used to *stand* next to her every day at the bus stop. Now that he *knows* her, how does this *standing* differ from the old days? Suddenly, this verb *to stand* has traveled miles.

Just before Valentine's Day, she isn't surprised that he wants to buy something nice for Kate. He knows just what he wants and has been saving money from baby-sitting jobs. He just needs her to drive him to the candy store uptown.

"No problem," she says. "We'll go after school."

They are having fun. She loves being invited into her son's

life for such errands. In the car, she asks him if he has enough money for his purchase and he shows her the twenty-dollar bill. Whew. More than enough, she thinks. This girl is only thirteen, after all. The street is crowded. No place to park. She pulls up in front of the store, double-parks, and tells him to hop out, she'll just drive around the block. "I'll pick you up in ten minutes."

"Thanks, Mom. You're great." Oh, what a sweetie. That's her son.

Five minutes later, she pulls back around to the front of the store and sees him standing outside already. Hmmm. He's not holding a shopping bag.

"What's up?" she asks as he opens the door.

"I need more money," he says.

"More money?" she says, unable to hide her frustration. "Twenty dollars should be plenty. What are you buying her?"

"It's a cute teddy bear holding a bag of candy," he explains. Leaning into the open door, he's obviously determined. "I need you to loan me ten dollars more."

"Can you get in the car?" she asks. Behind her, drivers are being forced to go around and she doesn't want to create a traffic jam. Sliding into the front seat, he looks piqued. Now, taking off for her second trip around the block, she tries to dissuade him from spending so much. Kate is not expecting such an expensive gift, she reasons. This girl may even be embarrassed by such a show of affection. Does he know if she is even planning to get him a gift in return? He doesn't want her advice. That much is plain to see. She pushes onward anyway. "How about a nice box of chocolates?" she suggests.

"A box of chocolates!" he repeats without turning his head to look at her. Big mistake. She might have suggested that he give her a ballpoint pen, judging by his reaction to this suggestion. Coming around the corner to the front of the store again, he finally faces her, with an expression she will come to know better and better during his adolescence: a cool, unmistakable "Butt out of it, Mom" stare.

"It's my money and I will pay you back when we get home but I need ten dollars more and I want to get this for her. That's that."

Stung silent, she pulls a ten from her wallet and hands it to him. There are no thanks in the uncomfortable air. When he opens the car door to step out onto the curb, it hits her: She's been replaced. Pleasing his girlfriend has become more important than pleasing her. Seventh-grade love or not, this is a tough place to be.

The next day, Valentine's Day, she opens a card with his seventh-grade teeny-tiny scrawl, which reads, "You are the best mother in the world for me." Catching her breath, stifling the mix of unshed tears from yesterday, she changes her mind: This is not such a tough place to be after all.

Two weeks later, she asks him, "How's Kate?"

"Oh, we broke up. She goes with Paul now."

The Art of
Hanging In There

....

"Women make the best bee-keepers because they have a special ability to love creatures that sting. It comes from years of loving children and husbands," explains one of the characters in Sue Monk Kidd's wonderful novel *The Secret Life of Bees*. I was so stunned by the wisdom in this observation that I pulled out a pen and had to write it down... right there in the airport in Indianapolis. The mother in this next story knows intimately what it feels like to be stung by her son. What's interesting about her is that she resisted the natural inclination to get out of harm's way by retreating during several emotionally dark years when he exhibited antisocial and self-destructive behaviors and his verbal attacks nearly killed her.

Olga Silverstein, a therapist and author of *The Courage to Raise Good Men*, would have applauded this mom. Women are encouraged to pull away from their boys during adolescence. Though there is mounting evidence to topple this theory, in some analytic circles, it is still said that one of the main tasks for a growing boy is to separate from his mother. "The taboo against closeness takes on new force," Silverstein says. And for a mom, "the fear of 'contaminating' her adolescent son with her own femininity" can be real. Dads sometimes encourage this concern. "Any lingering closeness must be put to an end," Silverstein reports, or your boy's masculinity could suffer. As a mother of a son herself, she adds, "We do this out of love for our sons—we want them to fit in, to be accepted, to succeed and thus, to be happy. But twenty years of looking at the results in the consulting room have convinced me that the costs are too high." Silverstein would have loved the way my friend hung in there.

Ride Alongside His Turmoil

She tells me, "Ninth grade was the roughest year." He's seventeen now and has just discovered something pretty amazing about himself. I'll get to that later. "That freshman year, he changed dramatically from a sweet, cuddly, caring, thoughtful, sensitive, funny person into a dark, nasty, selfish, cruel, heartless one." She has all these adjectives right there ready to offer because she's been keeping a journal, which probably helped her stay sane. Now, from a pleasant point in their relationship, it's a wonder and a comfort to glance back on his bad behavior. The ride through this adolescent hormonal and behavioral storm has been wild.

She tells me, "Most of his aggressions were directed at me but sometimes toward his siblings, his older brother and younger sister. He'd say things like, 'You don't like me'; 'You punish me more than anyone'; 'She's a spoiled brat . . . you let her do whatever she wants'; 'I hate you.' "

That hate line came up a lot. One day when she walked into his bedroom to ask him something, he demonstrated just how bizarrely he could behave. Try to picture yourself in the same situation. There she is, standing in the center of his room, speaking to him. He looks past her, making no eye contact and refusing to acknowledge her presence in his domain. He says, "I hear someone talking but I don't see anyone. I guess I'll leave." Easy to laugh about it now, but at the time, she was so swept back by his intent to hurt her, she just couldn't see his adolescent antics in any funny light at all. He walks around her without a glance and goes out the door.

She's not stupid and reads as much as she can about these predictable boyhood dramas. Friends share similar setbacks. Her other son is the little brother who arrived right after her first boy, a kid who has never given her a word of back talk or trouble. She may have even said to this kid who is torturing her, "Why can't you be more like your brother?" And oh brother, that could certainly make him want to take the opposite path through adolescence, the one clearly marked "trouble." His little sister's arrival when he was in grammar school and had been her baby for so many years may have contributed to his current chaos. Perhaps he felt rejected or that he had been replaced. Stop that, she says, this is the baby who's been difficult from day one. Meanwhile, the counselor at school even told her that this boy can be downright pleasant company in the classrooms and hallways. So what gives here? Is it only his family that he hates? When she is around, he's carrying daggers. It would be so easy to stay out of his sight and his life to save her sanity. But she explains, "Not a chance was I going to do that. I was along for the ride."

Reading books about adolescent psychology can make you even more confused about a boy's behavior, can't it? Sometimes you feel you need a professional voice of reason right there in person. So she finds a therapist who specializes in teenagers, and insists that he go. Resentful and barely speaking for months except in grunts, monosyllables, and snide grimaces, he actually keeps these appointments.

No one knows her son as well as she does, but what a comfort it was for that bumpy section. Even though she sensed deep down that not much was changing as a result of all the therapy, she was sleeping more soundly, thinking that someone else, someone who should know more than she did about psychology, was shouldering the burden. But don't get too comfortable. He's a smart kid.

Three months into his counseling sessions, she and her husband are invited to sit in on an appointment. What a surprise. In the session, she realizes that her son has not been telling his therapist the truth. So much for expertise . . . and this is a man with two degrees, someone who was supposed to know more than a mother!

Later, when she confronts her son about his lies, he says, "The guy needed to hear some juicy stories." Then he adds, "I don't want anyone poking around my life."

Cut to three years later. This son and this mother are cleaning the house on a Saturday for the tenth weekend in a row. She has pulled her old journal—the one she kept religiously when he was torturing her—from a desk drawer. She can't resist paging back to those bad old ninth-grade days, reading a few instances out loud to him as he scrubs the tub in her master bath nearby.

"Did I really do that?" he asks.

"Yes, you were perfectly capable of doing the most hurtful things," she admits. "Can you imagine how easily you lied to the therapist?"

"God, Mom, what a weirdo I was," he says.

"You weren't weird at all. It was perfectly normal behavior. A lot of boys that age, oh, about fourteen, fifteen, sixteen, just need to prove they are strong, tough, wild, reckless and they don't need a mom anymore. Raging hormones certainly add to your confusion. You really did act like you hated the whole family and me especially. But I never doubted that you'd come back around."

"Thanks, Mom." Then he remembers the scenes with his therapist. "You know, it was kind of fun playing straight into that guy's textbook-case imagination, though."

"You were so bad." She laughs, grabbing the vacuum and heading out into the hallway. He will follow along soon enough—right after he finishes the floor, in fact.

"What happened?" I ask.

"We just hung in there and kept on working at this relationship. We did find another therapist at one point. And I had him change schools, too, to get him out of his older brother's orbit. Eventually the hormonal storm died down as well."

"Okay, but how did he end up helping you clean house?"

"Actually, I was helping him clean that day," she admits. "It was a speeding ticket."

"What do you mean?"

"He needed money to pay the fine, but what both of us got from his eighty-eight miles an hour in a thirty-five zone was much more."

When his older brother earned a driver's license, she and her husband made a rule that any traffic violations or tickets would have to be paid by the boys themselves. They thought the personal sacrifice might hammer home a stronger message than if they offered to pick up the tab for a mistake. And it worked. His older brother had only one ticket in the two years he was a driver living at home. Now away at college, that son was still just as cautious about cars and wasting his money.

When this younger one got his first ticket, it was a whopper, at 88 miles per hour in a 35 zone. More than 50 miles over the limit is pretty scary. He managed to hold on to the license but to pay his parents back for the fine, he needed a job with flexible hours: housecleaning. His basketball team schedule didn't allow room for very much else.

Unsatisfied with her cleaning lady, she had taken over the work herself. She hated it. As it turned out, he surprised himself by loving it. Not only was the pay good, but he could do it his way, on his own time.

"Even after he paid us back for his fine, he kept right on cleaning. I kept paying him, too. He's such a good kid now that if it weren't for the journal, I might be tempted to think his turmoil during early adolescence was fiction. But it was the truth. The cleaning, though, isn't that still amazing?" she asks. "I'm going to miss him when he goes off to college next fall," she says.

"You're going to miss him or your clean house?"

"Both." She laughs.

The truth is, stereotypical thinking about what's expected of mothers during their sons' adolescence isn't ever the best route. You aren't a stereotype and neither is he. Trust yourself and hang in there during times of turmoil.

The Art of
Biting Your Tongue

We all know that the female brain operates in significantly different ways from the male brain. (Don't say this too loudly in mixed company. Don't imply that this fact means we are more intellectually or emotionally gifted, please—unless you want to lay down a gauntlet, and that's okay, too, at times.) Some of these findings are well documented, and many have emerged as a result of all the research funding in the nineties, deemed the Decade of the Brain by the National Institutes of Health (NIH).

Did you know that estimates place the number of brain cells in a man at 4 billion and those in women slightly lower? Yet, in intelligence testing, women generally score about 3 percent higher than men.

Standardized testing, statistical analyses, and good news about Parkinson's and Alzheimer's diseases, multiple sclerosis, and other deep brain disorders in medical journals are all very well. Some of my own interviews with neurologists, neurosurgeons, and clinical researchers doing exciting work on the cutting edges of brain dysfunction have made my heart race thinking of what might lie way out there on the futuristic edge of medicine. However, there is nothing like a little empirical evidence to make a mom sigh in serious concern about a son. As the Dolans of Satellite Sisters, National Public Radio fame, say in their book *Uncommon Senses,* "You need only to watch your brother attempt to cook fish sticks by putting them in a wood-handled frying pan and then putting the whole pan under the broiler to know that men are no more qualified to run the world than women are."

In this story, a smart mom wins a war by knowing when to bite her tongue and walk away from a battle of wits with her son.

Search for Signs of Intelligent Life

She walks out to the garage, takes a shocked, hard look at their Land Cruiser, and goes back inside. It's summer. Her nineteen-year-old son, a big (six-feet-four), troublesome sweetheart, is home from college after a successful freshman year and used the car over the weekend to visit friends on Cape Cod. Now the front right fender is hanging off; the left fender is crushed; and there's a banged-up area near the back.

She wakes him from a deep sleep.

"Wake up. Wake up."

"What's wrong, Mom?"

"What happened to the car?"

"What car?"

"Our car. Our Land Cruiser?"

"What do you mean?" he asks. "I drove it home last night."

"I guess you did, but didn't you notice anything wrong or missing?"

Now she's worried. Could he have been in an accident and not even known it? Is he on drugs? Was he drunk?

"Are you hungover? What were you doing?" she asks, looking at him closely for signs of health risks. She smells his breath. It's kicking, but that could just be from deep sleep and the bacteria that ferment overnight on a regular basis.

"What were you doing last night? I need to know right now."

"No, no, it's nothing like that. I'm fine. I had a few beers early. I'm tired, I guess, because it was late when I got to bed," he explains. "Honestly, I wasn't drunk. I wouldn't do that."

"But the car! It looks like it's been used as a battering ram. How could . . . ?"

"Really?" he asks, quite casually. "It was in the parking lot."

"A parking lot?" she asks, aghast. Is he a numbskull? What is he thinking?

"But all that damage . . . Have you looked at it?" she asks him.

"Well, it was dark."

Minutes later in their garage at the rear of the house, he whistles. "This baby has taken a beating."

"What happened?" she asks.

"I dunno."

Someday, they might just laugh about this. Today she can't. Today she is about to scream. Honestly. But she doesn't. And this is a woman who knows how to be furious to the point of irrationality. In fact, over the years, he has learned how to shut her down by simply saying nothing and letting her rage run over him. He's not dumb at all and actually scored a 1550 on those SATs. When they battle about his behavior, he often plays the "I dunno" card to win.

She bites her tongue and walks away, thinking, I will deal with him later. Harsh words will get her nowhere right now. Silence is a much better tool. It might even allow him time to reconstruct the events of his evening. She'll call his dad to cry now.

Raising this kid has taught her a few tricks for unearthing truths. When she is angry, as she is this morning, she's just not in good enough shape to win. Her son can make her so crazy with his escapades that in searching for signs of intelligent life, she's learned to stop and ask herself: Am I preoccupied, hungry, furious, frustrated, or just too tired to think straight? Later, she can go full speed ahead and plan a productive course of action for keeping him alive. But not now.

The Art of Being Content

This story makes me think of my friend Kay, who always used to say, "Success means different things to different people. Some parents might want to point to SAT scores, but to me, success means raising a contented human being—someone who contributes to society and enjoys being in the same room with me." You have to fight to be content with your kids, don't you? We want them to want what we want. That's only natural. But they may want something utterly discrete from our dreams.

On one wall of my living room hangs a framed calligraphic print, done by another old friend, who is a graphic artist. Carefully, back in the early seventies, when we were students at Penn State together, she penned the words of poet-philospher Kahlil Gibran into the shape of an arrow's point. Not only is it still beautiful after all these years, the message seems to underscore the lesson in this mom's regretful thinking. Gibran writes, "You are the bows from which your children as living arrows are sent forth. You may give them your love but not your thoughts. You may house their bodies but not their souls for their souls dwell in the house of tomorrow which you cannot visit, not even in your dreams. You may strive to be like them but seek not to make them like you. Your children are not your children. They are the sons and daughters of life longing for itself."

Accept Him

She's five feet two, a policewoman on the West Coast, and has trained at the Federal Bureau of Investigation. He is nearly nineteen, six feet three, two hundred pounds, a handsome, fun-loving, foolhardy boy. The girls have always loved him. Easily, always, he can make her cry and keep her stomach in knots. Isn't it true that you can be oh so strong physically—since she runs and lifts weights—but emotionally fragile as far as kids go? Even now, as he reaches the end of adolescence and rounds a bend into maturity, a friend's words, "But wait, there's more," play like a cautionary mantra, keeping her just steps shy of old pins and needles.

"He is very intelligent but doesn't believe it," she explains. "He doesn't actually think he's stupid, either, if that makes sense. He just refused to apply himself in high school, doing okay but not great. His teachers would always tell us that he had the ability, didn't cause major problems in class, but wouldn't work. Math," she recalls, "well, he excelled in math. He never listened to me." She's thinking of the time right after graduation, when he refused to go on to college.

"Why?" she wonders. "Why?" Why wouldn't he take these offers and run into his adult life more prepared than he is?

"He was so athletically gifted from the time he was little," she says. "He could throw and catch balls, Frisbees, anything, everything, and in baseball, well, his talents were right up there with the pros, but not his desire." Sigh. Sadness. Lost opportunities we can't take in our children's places. You know where she is mentally, in that land of regret. "I cried and cried and cried. Here was a child so capable but so steadfast in his refusal to show interest in anything. My husband and I had to rethink our goals for him. You know," she admits, "as parents we always want our children to have more and achieve more than we did, but maybe what we should really want is for them to be happy and healthy." I agree. We commiserate on the way parents can push kids too hard and reach an overkill impasse. Yet, it's hard not to scream from the side of the ball field. And how could you not be ashamed when a son fails? Hiding disappointment is almost impossible. Automatically, you put yourself in your child's place and can't help but want the very best for him, especially if you are a hard-driving, fearless, successful mother in your own right. At times, you lay down laws just made to be broken and, ultimately, they break you, too.

"He's not like me at all. I got straight A's," she admits. "We would get his midterm reports and warning notices from teachers. His grades were really bad, so we would threaten sanctions if he didn't improve academically. Then, he'd work just barely enough to hang on, but it wasn't quite enough. During baseball season, when he was the star pitcher, his report card was just awful. The school's rules allowed him to keep on playing, but ours didn't, so my husband went straight over to the ball field and made him pack up his equipment and quit the team," she says. She cried. He cried. His dad cried. Was it the right move? Who knows now? Yet, wistfully, she says, "I loved watching my son play baseball. I have him on videotape in championships when he dominated the field, pitching, playing, all over. Awesome."

Now watch her rearrange her thoughts. Here is a kid who is funny, lovable, and easy to be with and who sends her e-mail love notes. When she spent several weeks at the FBI Academy in Virginia for training, he mailed off a Mother's Day card that read, "Someday I am going to listen. Honest." Yet, he gravitates toward danger easily, and he *doesn't* listen. This is a boy who has had so many vehicle scares and close calls in cars that she can hardly separate one lurching memory from another. As a policewoman with official powers, she used to run her own license checks on him, only to make sure she was aware of the tickets—from the 60 mph on quiet 35-mph streets to the 80-plus mph on freeways. Coming home from work one day for lunch in an unmarked police car, she watched him pull out of their driveway and take off at warp 9 speed in a 25-mph zone. "When I finally caught up with him at a stoplight, I wanted to drag him physically right out of that driver's-side window. I was so angry. He was grounded again and I don't think I even told his father because I was afraid of how furious he might be." His sister says that he spent his entire high school career grounded. Slight exaggeration? Maybe not.

Always waiting for that awful, mostly middle-of-the-night phone call, she was astonished to learn that he "rode a crotch rocket" while visiting his grandparents and uncle in California.

"Do you know what that is?" she asks.

I don't. Do I want to know? I need to, in order to understand this boy better.

"He laid his motorbike down on a freeway in rush-hour traffic and slid under a truck."

Ouch. I can almost feel her heart beating; the memory of this escapade hasn't grown any easier for her to recall, even with a two-year distance. "Scraped up, but thank God, he wasn't killed. His bike was totaled—perhaps it was for the best, because he is certainly not the kind of kid who needs one. The strange part about it was that his uncle passed the accident on the other side of the freeway but wasn't aware that he knew the boy strapped to the board with the paramedics. Oh, God. My son."

Some mothers' stories about their sons' walks on the wild side make us breathe sighs of relief, happy that we haven't had to travel in such shoes. Others offer kinship. Some make you feel uncomfortably sad, even though they weren't meant to.

"That crotch rocket was no big deal for him. He used to lower the body of his truck so close to the roadbed that he once hit railroad tracks with the undercarriage. He was lucky not to be seriously hurt that time either. Why would he do that? Why wouldn't he listen?"

A pause and laughter move her forward to a recent e-mail in which he describes himself as a fearless mama's boy because he's not afraid to admit to anyone how much he loves her. Back in grade school and even in junior high, he was proud of himself because she depended on him when she practiced her self-defense tactics. Lately, though it's no longer true because he is so strong, he still tells friends that his mom can "whip his ass."

"I don't try to change his mind about that," she says, "though I did tell him he was delusional when he said he's had an idyllic childhood and we are the best parents in the world."

"You are the best, bester, maybe even the bestest mother," he writes. Was he joking? Of course not. She smiles, because she knows that he's as honest in these matters as she is.

Here is the kind of woman who braves a career in police work and who is unafraid of dangers you and I would certainly do our best to dodge. She is someone who can go fearlessly after suspects in triple-murder cases. I know because she told me about one. Her son may be just as fearless in his own way, though apparently not yet as driven toward professional or financial success as she has been.

The truth is, regrets about what she might have done differently in raising her boy or why he isn't on someone else's definition of a fast track aren't necessary. He loves her. She loves him. Proof of her mothering success—not only does he like being in the same room with her, he keeps her on his e-mail buddy list as well.

The Art of Rescue

O f all the species, we humans take the longest for our brains to fully mature," Daniel Goleman writes in his best-seller, *Emotional Intelligence*. "Several brain areas are among the slowest to mature. While the sensory areas mature during early childhood and the limbic system by puberty, the frontal lobes—seat of emotional self-control, understanding and artful response—continue to develop into late adolescence, until somewhere between sixteen and eighteen years of age."

In this story, that immature brain may be the only explanation a mother can swallow for her son's stupidity. Many of us have had to rescue a boy caught in a web of deceit or failure. We only hope that time is on his side and he will eventually learn self-control. Perhaps being made to suffer the consequences of his actions can stimulate some of those frontal-lobe areas in the brain to mature, too. That's what this mom is waiting for.

Go to School

He is fifteen. She is not happy at all. Not until she reaches Room 213, eighth-period English class on Back to School Night at the high school does it really sink in. I mean really, seriously, that's when the churning in the pit of her stomach begins. You know the feeling of awful disbelief that can gnaw, rumble, and grumble a passage all the way through an anxious body? Oh God. Oh how could he? By this time, it is nearly 9:30 and her day has been long already. Showing six houses to picky prospective buyers, she should be dead tired and dragging. Yet anger has her blood pumping furiously. A cup of lukewarm old-coffeepot coffee in the cafeteria during *his* fifth-period "lunch" hasn't helped her state of anxiety either.

The puzzle began back in his fourth period, just about midpoint in an evening she had been anticipating not with dread but with enthusiasm. She's co-president of the Parent Teacher Student Organization, or PTSO, a position into which she was dragged by a really good friend at a time in the previous school year when no other parents would step forward. "C'mon," she was cajoled, "we really need to do this. Not only will we be performing a service for the school and volunteering to be one of those points of light the politicians applaud, but we'll be able to get a real sense of what's happening right inside the high school walls." This last possibility was, obviously, the most seductive. After all, though both of her boys could be classified as good kids, neither had ever chosen to jump through those educational hoops held high by the AP teachers and administrators anxious to raise standardized test scores. The principal was elated to have not one but two willing workers free of charge.

Now, in mid-October, she knows so many of these high

school teachers by sight and by reputation. This is her chance to hear them describe exactly what's happening in the class-rooms. Hmmmm. So what's been happening? Not much.

In geometry class, right before her son's scheduled lunch break, Mr. L. looks surprised to see her sit down in the second row. "I had a really nice time at the Welcome Back breakfast you served. Thanks so much. You know, we may not say it all the time, but we teachers do appreciate the efforts some parents make on our behalf."

Then . . .

"But I don't think your son is in my class," he says bluntly.

"That's funny. He's got you right here on his Back to School Night class schedule," she explains. A rush-rush blanket of con-fusion usually clouds these once-a-year parental excursions into High School Land, so she doesn't think too much of the matter. She's just a little surprised. Then, by class end, her sur-prise turns to frustration. Being co-president of the PTSO was supposed to have rubbed a little recognition off on her entire family, not just her. Forget about it, she tells herself. This is nothing to get excited about. Not to worry.

Yet, she can't concentrate on talk of geometry, class policy for missed homework assignments, and how that breakdown for grading will go.

Fifth period, she drinks coffee and chats with other parents in the first-floor cafeteria. She dismisses the little storm warn-ing voice inside her head. After checking on the volunteers at the PTSO table in the front hallway, where school calendars are being offered in a fund-raising effort, she goes up the stairs and down the hall to the science wing.

Now, in sixth period, Dr. L. tells her that certainly her son must have switched out of this particular biology section. "Could be in Mr. O.'s class. Better ask in the science depart-ment office." Hmmmm. Why didn't anyone ever tell her? she wonders. Could he have dropped this class completely without telling her? Maybe he forged her signature on the card.

Seventh period, she arrives for Italian II way up in 318, only to discover that it is a remedial math class, not Italian at all. How could he have put Room 318 on the form? She rereads his handwritten Back to School Night schedule completed in homeroom period that very day. Out in the hall, with no one to ask and only twenty minutes allotted for each mini-class parent session, she never does locate that seventh-period Italian II class. Skip it. Go to eighth period and get this over with.

By this last period of the evening, she has no doubt. She doesn't even ask Mr. A. about her child's behavior. She knows that Mr. A. has never seen him step foot inside Room 213.

Nearly six weeks into his sophomore year, he is in big, big trouble. Just thinking about it makes her feel nauseous. Don't throw up. Don't throw up. Keep that coffee down. The school policy for excused absences permits only nine days out, and whatever he's been doing, there is no excuse possible. Trying to count how many days have passed since that first week in September or to recall the passage on cutting classes in the student handbook (page 10, which she helped write, by the way), she fidgets for her cell phone at the bottom of her pocketbook. Should she call now or surprise him later? Is his father home yet? Obviously, he must know what's coming. Yet he was so calm when she went out the door earlier that evening. "You look nice, Mom," he had said. What a master of deception he is. Whew . . . now she remembers all those earnest answers to her questions about how school was going. Fine. Fine. No problem.

" 'Bye, Mom," he had hollered. What is he thinking? Has he been thinking at all? Rarely antagonistic, obnoxious, or even disdainful of adult authority, with dark eyes, a boyishly handsome face, and an ever-ready mischievous grin, he is a mystery.

There is no way in the world she would ever have been able to cut classes week after week. The fear of being found out would have made her physically ill even at his age.

The desk chair is so uncomfortable that she can hardly sit still these last fifteen minutes in an English class on an October evening that can't end too soon. Caught between fury with her son, anger at a school that would let such a thing—wait a minute, this is no inanimate thing or piece of paper, this is her child—slip through, she is deflated. Hours and hours of energy have been poured away and out of her life. She could have been selling houses, not typing PTSO minutes. Bright, personable, artistically gifted, unwilling to please just for the sake of pleasing, he keeps pulling himself into nightmare directions. He is just so adamant about not buying into the notion of sacrificing a little freedom in the present tense in order to gain the most opportunity in the future that she simply can't believe it. Where does this stupidity come from? Her side of the family? Or her husband's? She thinks about the man she married, the father of her two children. He's a successful engineer and could never be considered stupid. Her mind flits to her son's insistence on taking no advanced placement courses. Art may be the only class on his agenda he really has been attending.

At home, he hears her come in the side door. Uh-oh.

He looks at her. She has been crying.

"What have you been doing all these afternoons?"

"Well, not much," he admits. "I dunno."

To be honest, once he climbed into the game of five lunch periods in a row and proceeded to repeat his crime twenty-eight times, he just, well, he just didn't know how to dig himself out. In fact, he has been waiting for her to lend him a hand.

"What are we going to do?" she asks him.

He gives her a tissue. "I dunno."

"Well, I do," she says, and they start to laugh. After all, she's the PTSO co-president, and that *might* buy them a little power.

"How could you?" she says, shaking her head, rolling her eyes, and reaching out to him.

"I dunno."

The truth is, sometimes there are no easy solutions, but having a presence in the high school will definitely help her sort the way through this mothering maze. She'll be able to rescue him. Somehow.

The Art of
Making the Last Move

In his wonderfully honest, zany advice to adolescent boys, Jeremy Daldry tells his boy readers of *The Teenage Guy's Survival Guide: The Real Deal on Girls, Growing Up, and Other Guy Stuff,* that girls "are great. We love them. But that doesn't stop girls from being the cause of more heartache, confusion, and sleepless nights than almost anything else." His words of wisdom could easily be aimed at us, the mothers of love-struck adolescent boys. We worry when they aren't making enough connections with the opposite sex. And then we turn around and sometimes have to worry about the connections they *are* making.

The mother in this story has her wish for her son come true and then watches it turn into her version of a nightmare. Feeling powerless to exert any influence over him at first, in the end she manages to make a surprising last move. She proves that she is not without resources even when confronted with a revolution in her home. And her actions sweetly let both her boys know that, yes, she does know best occasionally.

Follow Your Instincts

He's seventeen, and she's happy that he has finally found a girl-friend. It's not that he didn't ever get along with girls before that, she tells me. There were moments, sidelong glances, school hallway crushes, a few mysterious phone calls here and there in the early teens. What about that eighth-grade social? At one point, she knows he was smitten with long-haired Alexa, because he spent a sunny afternoon, fully clothed, in bed after his first "Dear John" phone call. No tears. Just a strange, strained look and a series of cryptic *I'm okay*s and *Leave-me-alone*s. He just wasn't very good at reading girls' signals. Apparently, he also found it hard to believe that girls would really be romantically interested in him. He's been a bit of a quiet mystery.

She sighs. "I used to worry about him and wonder if he would ever have a real social life or how involved I should be to make this happen." Is this our job? Of course not. But well, maybe, sometimes. On occasion, don't they invite us to share at the same time they shut us out? Whoa. Pull in, push away is the name of this game most moms know. She thinks back. Was it up to her to help him get a date for that junior prom he didn't attend last year? She could have. She would have. She has friends with willing daughters. Oh, how she had wanted him to go, to grab every experience high school has to offer. Yet, he was monosyllabic back then, with body language screaming, "Stay out of it, Mom." His older brother hands her no such dilemmas when it comes to these traditional rites of passage. How can two sons from the same body—HERS—with the same genetic code be so different? This boy is—or was—different. Now it's happened—he's got this girlfriend—and she wishes it hadn't.

"It was definitely time," she recalls. "He had his driver's license. He had bought a car. Wasn't a girlfriend the next step?"

"Sure." I nod. "I guess."

"Well, I suppose I wasn't expecting the complete transformation in him as a result of this girl."

"What do you mean?"

"He would do anything for her. I mean, anything to be with her. I really had nothing against her, but I hated the person my son had become. He was staying out until four A.M. with this girl, night after night. I was a wreck. I'd be waiting in my bathrobe at the door when he came in. My husband thought I was crazy. Was I? Am I?"

"I don't think so."

"This kid was still in high school. I was really, really a wreck, spending far too much time thinking about him, and he knew it." When face-to-face with her worry, he'd just hang his head and say, "I have no excuse." Still polite, still her son, but not really.

Even after listening earnestly to her complaints, to her logic, and to her threats of punishment, he'd do the very same thing the following night.

"Whatever this girl was offering was worth more to him than whatever his actions were doing to me," she recalls.

She remembers a scene on a school morning more than a decade ago, when she had two toddlers and a baby on her hip in the hallway outside the elementary auditorium. "His class files by before we can find our seats inside. We stand there and he sees us. We all beam and wave, even the baby. Then he looks back at the little boy behind him in line and says loudly, proudly, 'That's my mom.' "

She stops here for a second, feeling a little teary. "I can still see his face today, and it makes me want to cry."

She wouldn't have thought his behavior at seventeen could get much worse, but it does. One night she never got to bed at all, not even at 4 A.M. Everyone else was asleep—including her husband, whose laissez-faire approach to their son's season of adolescent sex is driving her nuts. "I was up watching television, as usual, waiting for him to call or come home when the phone rings, pretty early, a little after midnight," she says.

"It's me," he says.

"Where are you?" she asks.

"I'm at Julie's house and I wanted to let you know that I'm sleeping over."

Though she has been on this road with him for weeks, she still can't imagine his bravado, that male moxie tossed right up into her face, shocking her a little senseless. So she screams, which is unlike her. She's not a screamer. "What? Why? Where are her parents? What's happened?"

He's very calm. He's feeling his power. "Nothing's happened. Her parents are here, asleep. She isn't feeling well and I don't want to leave her."

Probably drunk, this mom's mind flashes. Don't say it. That accusation about Julie will only make matters worse. Hold back. Don't go near another scream.

"I want you to come home now," she says, trying to control herself. Calm. Calm. Steady. "It's not appropriate for you to sleep over at your girlfriend's house. You are only in high school."

"It's not like that, Mom. Besides, I don't feel like getting up and driving home."

Julie's house is not more than ten city-length blocks away. Hmmmm.

"I'll come over and get you," she offers.

"No, you're making way too big of a deal about this," he says. "I will see you in the morning."

Click. He hangs up.

"What's a mother supposed to do?' she asks. "I mean really?"

I don't know. I haven't been in that particular spot, I tell her.

"Do I drive over there? Wake up Julie's family? Drag my son out of his girlfriend's bed? Which is what I wanted to do."

She shakes her head, drinks some water, realizes she is powerless. "Looking back, it still surprises me that I didn't go over there. The urge to go somewhere, do something, take control of an uncontrollable situation was so overpowering."

She sits in the chair, furious that he has hung up on her, asking herself over and over again where she went wrong. How could he do this? She didn't raise a boy who could be so defiant. What was the world coming to?

"I never got out of that chair. Seriously," she says. "I felt like there must be something I could do. I just felt so stuck."

As the sun comes up, she starts to doubt her sanity and wonders if she should believe her husband, who has been saying all along that there isn't anything they can do about this and that boys will be boys, especially at seventeen and in love. Is this the way of the world now? All the kids on the TV show *Dawson's Creek* sleep over and it is all very innocent, most of the time. Still, she's in new territory here and without a map, that's for sure.

"I guess I should have been grateful that he called me to say where he was and that he wasn't coming home," she admits to me. In the morning, still swinging emotionally between anger and acceptance, she isn't happy with her husband, who just says, "What are you going to do in a few months when he is away at college and can stay out all night if he wants? Are you going to sit up in chairs for the next four years?"

Of course not. We moms are a flexible breed for the most part. What's troubling about the trap of her night is the sense that there is nothing she can do, that she has no power to protect or keep her son safe. Then she has a thought, a really good idea, a plan that offers her a platform of action. She grabs it gratefully. This is a small step, you might even want to call it silly, but her statement is so happily definitive. I clap my hands in approval. Good going.

After dinner, both sons discover the results of her decision in the bathroom medicine chest they share upstairs. Still in the kitchen, loading the dishwasher, she turns as the older one taps her on the shoulder.

"Hey Mom? Look what we found."

Smiling sheepishly, the seventeen-year-old is standing behind his brother, as usual.

"Is this your doing?" his brother asks her, laughing as he holds up several packages of condoms.

She grins for the first time all day. A powerful smile.

"Well, I felt like I had to *do* something," she answers. "They are for both you guys, in fact."

Like gunslingers, who know they can drop their gun belts in a duel that is over, she and her seventeen-year-old start to laugh really hard.

The older one says, with the condoms still in his hand, "You two are crazy."

No, they aren't, especially not her.

The truth is, buying condoms was her way of taking back a bit of the control she had lost in the household. She may not be ready for either of them to have sex, but if they are and she can't stop them, as she has learned, then she'll make sure they take precautions.

The Art of
Exercising Good Judgment

"What at four in the afternoon seems challenging, at four in the morning is grueling," says Marc Brown, M.D., in his book *Emergency! True Stories from the Nation's ERs.* Oh, do moms know that sensation well! The mother in this story knows intimately what it feels like to be awakened at 4:00 A.M. by a telephone call and the sound of a police officer's voice. Routinely, her son acts first and thinks later, especially when he is playing with his best friend, a kid who also acts first and thinks later.

You can lock such a boy up—figuratively speaking—and become an expert in punishment. But you might kill your relationship by taking that approach. Is that what you really want? What's more, lines drawn in fear and rules made in anger may not teach him anything but how much he wants to escape. Meanwhile, when you let worry control your mothering moves, you can rob your son of opportunities to develop good judgment. Mistakes get made all the time. On the other hand, discipline can have a positive effect on a boy, as this mom began to see. Everyone needs discipline. It is only through discipline that I can finish writing a book. Think positive discipline, not negative punishment. That's what this mom did.

Try Discipline

This is a story that should start in your bed. Go there for a second in your imagination. To love sleeping soundly all night long, especially in late summer, is your inalienable right. This is a warm night when the temperature drops to a perfectly peaceful spot on the thermometer and a light, barely curtain-breaking breeze sweeps across your face, making your dreams detour to Caribbean vacations. . . . Well, there's nothing wrong with that, is there? Please don't interrupt.

She, in fact, has just invested money in a new comforter-and-sheet set on sale at Wal-Mart. It was top of the line and the high thread count resting on her skin, the fact that bills had been paid that day in full, and that there are no fires to be put out at work in the doctors' office she manages all conspire to allow her one of those really, really restful occasions you just don't have very often when you are the mother of a teenage boy. Now figure this into the equation as well: Isn't it true that in the summer, you're not as worried about school-related issues? There's no homework due. There are no standardized tests on the immediate horizon to make everyone in the household crazy with dread. There are no midterm warnings arriving in the mail. The breakneck September-to-June schedule eases. By mid-August, unless he's in preseason football or soccer training, and worried about making the team, you can think to yourself: Well, there is nothing major to worry about tonight. Go ahead, fall fast asleep, and stay there until at least 6:00 A.M. when the alarm goes off.

Let me tell you that this fifteen-year-old is not a big drinker, so she isn't even focusing on drunken spills on this particular Tuesday. Think about it: He doesn't drive cars yet. He's a quirky kid, kind of fearless, with lots of "whatever" responses to her interrogations about his thoughts, his intentions, his goals. He does get himself into trouble and has not been an easy child to parent, that's for sure. Her two daughters never insisted on wearing socks on the beach to walk across the sand. Nor did they sleep on the floor of her bedroom next to her side for a couple of preschool years of their lives. Perhaps that's why she can fall into bed easier as he has grown older and accustomed to his own bed. She doesn't need to think about stepping over him on a trip to the bathroom in the middle of the night. This boy has certainly taught her the biological, psychological, and social meaning of the word *flexible*. That's an adjective she easily accepts and applies to herself now, thanks to him. Lately, though, she's been thinking that he needs something else from her besides her easygoing approach. But what? All he can say in answer to her questions is "Whatever."

Tonight he isn't even home. He's sleeping over at his friend Aaron's house with a group of guys. These kids aren't exactly nerds, nor are they in the fast crowd. She'd put them somewhere in between, and her oldest daughter agrees.

"They are just a little weird, Mom," she's been told. "But don't worry. A lot of boys his age are kind of squirrelly strange. I see them in the halls at school all the time. Even my own brother won't acknowledge me sometimes." She wishes he were more like his sisters. They seem to be able to set their own boundaries and then stay within the lines of good behavior.

Her son and his friend Aaron have known each other for ages, since kindergarten, much to the chagrin of Aaron's parents, especially the dad, who would prefer the kids take separate paths. It's not a religious thing, she knows, although Hebrew classes for Aaron and confirmation sessions for her son took them into separate after-school directions during middle school. They like each other. Religious background would never tear them apart, and they live in a town where residents wear their diverse cultural and religious backgrounds proudly, in fact. The trouble with these boys is that they are always getting into trouble. Together over the years, their problem is one she thinks of as drifting creatively into danger—and in the most outrageous ways. For the most part, there's been nothing malicious in their adventures, which is why she doesn't feel as strongly as Aaron's dad about the boys' being together. In second grade, they set a model train platform on fire in her basement. But they were only trying to create a smoke plume in the engine car. At ten, they decided to walk nine miles to the mall when no parent was available to drive them. Yet, wasn't Mother's Day that coming Sunday and the boys had shopping in mind? Dangerous but cute. Yet, oh no, she'll never forget the time they tried melting He-Man action figures in the microwave. She had to trash a really nice microwave oven as a result. They were lucky that the whole thing didn't blow up and hurt them.

Tonight, four boys are sleeping in Aaron's basement, so the deadly mix of their two minds may be diluted by two additional brains. That's good. All she said when dropping him off was "Be careful," biting her tongue from reminding him of the nightmares he and Aaron have in their historical friendship.

Aaron lives only ten blocks away. In fact, her son left his bicycle there earlier in the week, because he planned to pedal home in the morning when she would be at work. Summers are tough for working moms when teenagers are too old for adult supervision but not mature enough to think straight. Do you let the crowd hang out at your house when no parent is present? In her case, of course. But she worries, and their appetites make for expensive afternoons and messy cleanups. What are you supposed to do? He's too young to work and all the baby-sitting jobs go to girls. His two sports camps—a full week of baseball and five days of ice hockey—are finished. She and his dad drove all the way to Montreal so he could attend a special goalie program, where he and a friend learned how to curse in French.

"Do you think the boys are okay?" she asks her husband as they climb into bed at the deliciously early eleventh hour of a long day.

"Who knows?" he answers.

They laugh.

In Aaron's basement, under the Ping-Pong table where they have spread out sleeping bags, the boys are laughing, too. One of the guys noticed that golf carts parked up at the college in the north end of town behind the football stadium by the maintenance crew have their ignition keys hanging in plain sight, right in the vehicles, ready and waiting. The four grow hysterical laughing about how stupid college officials must be to be so cavalier and inviting. They talk and stare at the chewing gum wads stuck to the underside of the table. . . . Wouldn't it be fun to take a couple of carts and go for a spin around campus? Two have spent summer days caddying at a nearby country club and know all about such carts—a short driving step up from the bumper cars they all love on beach boardwalks.

By 2 A.M., there is no stopping the forward momentum of their open season on golf carts. They hop on bicycles and head north. One has to ride sidesaddle across her son's ten-speed. Tricky.

Four A.M. Fast asleep. The phone is on her side of the bed. It rings. She recalls that it had to be at least four times before she jumped to it, realizing that the sound wasn't in her dream. The answering machine picked up, so the voice on the phone was suddenly magnified and being recorded down in the kitchen. Damn. She can hear that curious echo of voices—the deep male one as well as her own—coming from the kitchen: a nightmare of sounds far from that Caribbean beach back in her deep-brain REM sleep.

"I couldn't believe it. Four o'clock in the morning," she tells me. "I had been out so cold and soundly that it took me several minutes to shake myself free from sleep. Then I could hear our voices coming from the kitchen as well as right there in my bed. You know how answering machines can do that if you pick up just as the incoming message is being recorded?"

"Sure, I do."

The officer identifies himself and asks, "Do you know where your son is?"

She answers, "Well he's supposed to be sleeping at his friend Aaron's house." Thudding fear. Is he dead? Is he injured? Where is he? Out of her warm, deep sleep, she is now in every mother's bad dream.

"The police officer was quite nice, considering the circumstances," she recalls. "He was okay. I started breathing again, sort of. Someone on Mountainview Avenue had called the station to report golf carts speeding up and down their street. The boys had taken their cart spree off the school's campus and onto side streets. The garbage cans at curbsides looked like fair play at the time."

"You can pick him up here at the station," she's told.

"We decided that I would go alone because my husband had to get up in another hour for his commute and I'm pretty good in these encounters. We were both afraid that he would lose his cool somewhere along the way. Meanwhile, I couldn't stop shaking. My brain was buzzing," she recalls. "You know that frantic kind of internal buzz you can get when something really bad is going wrong. Of course, he wasn't hurt physically and I think I was secretly, deep down relieved, but we were talking about possession of stolen property and all sorts of other bad stuff. Would we need a lawyer? The boys had tried to run away, so resisting arrest might also be a charge. I just didn't know. This was not even in the same league as basement fires and microwave meltdowns."

She pulls on her jeans, throws a big shirt over her favorite sleeping T, finds her flip-flops, pocketbook, and car keys. This is what moms do.

There is no traffic. Aaron's father is already there when she enters the building. You can see that he is furious and not just at Aaron. Oh, maybe a little of his wrath is directed toward his own son, but what galls her and stops her in her tracks immediately is not the policeman or the bowed heads of the boys on the bench but this adult's behavior toward her little boy.

"What the hell were you thinking?" he's demanding, looking straight at her child. "You need to be punished." Even the arresting officer is surprised. Punished? The police are going to do that, not this father who is out of control here.

"Wait a minute," she interrupts. "There are four boys here. Who do you think you are talking to?" Her voice is louder than she anticipated.

("I screamed at him," she tells me.)

Her scream—suddenly—shocks her son, who stands up tall. "Mom. Mom," he says. "It's okay. It's okay. Whatever."

"No, Aaron's dad is not acting okay. You didn't do this on your own."

A phone rings there behind the counter.

"No he didn't do it on his own," Aaron says, turning to his father. "It was nobody's idea, Dad. I mean, what I mean is that it was all four of us. Those keys hanging right there in the ignitions. We just started picturing what fun it might be and couldn't not do it."

"How stupid can you be?" Aaron's dad hollers, as if he had lost a few IQ points of his own there in the station. "Stupid. Stupid. Stupid."

Quietly, she grabs her son's hand and they walk to the counter to hear all about their next legal step. Her son is not stupid at all. He knows it.

"How are you?" she asks when they get into her car.

"Oh. Whatever."

"What is this 'whatever'?" she asks.

"You know," he says.

"No, I don't know. Are you okay?"

"Sure."

Yet, she doesn't really know if he is okay. In the morning, she'll call her office and take a personal day. She needs time to discuss her son's legal situation with her husband and possibly with a lawyer, but she also wants to start investigating that area of her boy's life lying beneath the "whatevers." She sees now that, at fifteen, he may need more discipline than she ever had to give the girls. To keep him playing within the lines of the law, she's not going to cut off his friendship with Aaron. Those boys could probably provide novelist Stephen King with a few rich details worth developing into story lines. Sleepovers this summer? Well, they have to be earned, not awarded automatically. And another course she'll pursue tomorrow is a phone call to Aaron's dad. That man was way out of line. What a tyrant, she thinks. But she won't say that to him. She just needs to talk about the boys' longstanding friendship. Don't worry. She knows how to exercise good judgment even if this dad and her son don't yet.

The Art of Winning

In an interview with a *New York Times* reporter, poet Maya Angelou offered one of her secrets for maintaining sanity. I've put the line up on my bulletin board so I can see it often, and be easily reminded of it, especially when I've made a crazy mistake. Copy this, especially if your son plays team sports where winning is everything and coaches are unchecked: "Laughing as much as possible. That's very important. You must laugh as much as you cry, just for balance."

Both of my children played a lot of athletics. Zach just gravitated naturally to soccer, baseball, and then ice hockey. He is still passionate about his games and plays roller hockey in a young men's league all year long. Maggie, twenty-two, is also a gifted athlete and excelled at soccer from kindergarten on. She played ice hockey, too, and managed to make co-captain on an all-boys' team once. However, she learned the hard way that even being the best she could possibly be couldn't always buy a nasty coach's esteem. Some

grown men just shouldn't be allowed near our children, don't you agree?

In this story, a mother lets a crazy coach's influence over her son lead them to a dangerous place.
She laughs about it now but did some crying at the
time, as Maya might recommend. Yet, in the end, this
boy knew how to win anyway.

▪ ▪

Sniff Out the Rats

He broke his leg on a Saturday night in January in the second
period of a high school ice hockey game when his skate got
caught in the opposing team's goalie's pads. She knew it. She
didn't know it. Sitting in the stands in the far corner of the
metal-cold bleachers across the ice, she saw him skate behind
the net wrapping around the corner post, with his stick low,
carrying the puck perfectly. A goal, she thought, this could be
the goal he needs to impress the new coach. Her son liked
those kinds of moves. At left wing, he rarely took hard slap
shots from the blue line, preferring instead to put his mark on
the scoreboard with sneaky, low, corner-of-the-net scores.

We are months away from that night now, but she takes me
back, trying to understand where her mother's instinct went.

This goalie is good, and when the boys collide in a jumble
of pads, sticks, and a net pulled off the pegs, her son's leg is
snagged, twisted strangely, and stuck somewhere. She knows
immediately that he's hurt.

Even from her vantage point, she can see the odd twist to
his leg. Someone gives him an arm and he pulls himself up.
Leaning on his stick, with a hand on his leg, he approaches the
safety of his team's bench very slowly, not attempting to hop

the waist-high boards. One of the managers opens the gate for him. Now, if you are the mother of an ice hockey player, you know boys just don't do that when they are almost seventeen, juniors in high school, and have been playing this crazy game for a decade. Over the boards is the only way to go . . . unless you are injured. He's hurt, she thinks. He's hurt.

Standing up now, with one foot already on the step below, balancing both her weight and her decision, she deliberates about whether to go and embarrass him in front of this talk-tough coach her son has been trying to impress all season. Pounding heart. Sweaty palms. Indecision. Should she stay put and wait to be summoned by the team's trainer? By the assistant? By someone who can see that her boy is seriously injured? What is he thinking now? Does he want her to run to his rescue? He's not her baby anymore and has told her that in myriad ways and words. She waits.

The mom next to her, Julie, is a veteran with three sons, a daughter, and her own decade invested in this dangerous game. Julie puts a hand on her coat sleeve and says, "Now, don't worry. I think he's okay. Wait a minute." A whistle blows. Time-out.

"The wait was endless," she recounts. "I held my breath and then everything seemed to be all right."

A few minutes later, he's back on the ice but not skating well. Clearly, he's dragging his left leg. What an utterly stupid situation, she thinks, commiserating with Julie. "Sometimes I think this game just stinks, don't you? I think we must be insane to put our kids into this."

"But they love it," Julie argues.

"I know. I know."

Her next thought: What a determined kid! He is in pain and she can feel it as well as see it as he glides past her now and to check a player on the opposing team at the boards right in her direct line of vision. He can't do it. There's no fire in his game.

"I was just one big knot the rest of that game and I didn't even care that they won," she explains.

Afterward, she is surprised to see him emerge from the locker room on two feet. He's walking. Maybe he's okay, she thinks.

"Hi, Mom," he says.

"Hey, what happened back there in the second period in front of the net?" she asks. "Did you hurt your leg?"

"Yeah. Kind of. I think I pulled something, but Coach says it's nothing," he explains. "The trainer wrapped it for me and said to ice it when I get home." He pulls up his baggy pant leg to show her how his knee has been tended. Not too bad. Okay. Okay. Together, they round the rink, walking toward the exit, while waving and talking to other parents and players.

"Nice game, nice game" is a repetitious refrain all around. Someone hollers to them, "You okay?" and he answers, "Sure, sure."

As a varsity player, he's entitled to leave his equipment behind in the high school team's locker room. That's been nice this year. Almost every other season in this ice hockey experience, they've dragged the big red bag home to air out in the garage. If you've never caught a whiff of a sweat-wet hockey bag full of padding and gear, you're lucky. The stink is so powerful that nothing eats it away, not powders, sprays, or odor-eaters of any kind.

Tonight, outside, as they head for the family car, she realizes that being able to leave the bag behind is more than a blessing for the nose. Certainly, he couldn't have carried it alone, for, beyond the eyes of his teammates, parents, and Coach; he can't walk. She puts her arm around his waist and he leans heavily on her as they struggle into the dark parking lot.

"This isn't good at all. Oh, honey, we've got to get you to the doctor's office right away," she says. "This is no sprain. What about Middleton's ER? Let's go now."

He is protest personified and vehement. "Mom, please, don't do that. I can't. I can't do that."

"What are you talking about? You are really hurt," she says, surprised by his reaction. "What happened?"

Here's the story: With teeth grinding and eyes narrowed angrily, the coach turned to him on the bench and said, "Don't you dare think this means you are going to miss your next shift!" Silence. Even the team's trainer is shocked. Then, "What a bunch of goddamn wimps. If we don't win this one, we won't be in the county playoffs. Jesus f-----g Christ. You guys suck. Wimps. Every one of you. Wimps."

"He's crazy, Mom," her son says. "I know that. Everyone knows it. But this is my team. I am not going to the hospital now. Besides, the trainer said it was just a sprain."

She is furious. Oh God. Caught between a rock and a hard place, she caves in to her son's determination. Her husband, always a voice of reason in the house, is gone until Wednesday on business. For tonight, at least, her will alone isn't enough to drown out the mix of macho fear, loyalty, and pride playing in this big boy's head.

"Let's just see what it looks like at home," she says.

In their family room, they ice the leg, which is starting to swell. Unwrapping the bandage, she can see that it's his knee, which doesn't appear to be broken or dislocated. He starts to feel better on painkillers and they go with the RICE formula: Rest, Ice, Compression, Elevation. On the couch with his leg propped up, he looks better. Maybe it is just a strain or sprain, she thinks. If it were broken or anything serious, wouldn't she know? Wouldn't the trainer have been able to detect it? Wouldn't her son be even further immobilized? Neither of her children has broken any bones. He's the oldest. Later, after he is asleep, she second-guesses her decision and pulls out the blue *Sports Medicine Bible,* which states: "By far the most common of acute knee injuries is the ligament strain." That's what it is, she reassures herself. Just a strain, a sprain. Can it wait until Monday? She'll call the orthopedist Julie uses first thing Monday morning and have him checked.

When her husband telephones later from California, the news of their son's injury is accepted with calm.

"These things are bound to happen," he says. "He's a boy. He'll be all right. You're doing the right thing."

"Are you sure? I don't know."

On Sunday, the leg is still painful and swollen. He stays on the couch, still insistent about avoiding any emergency doctor's opinion.

On Monday, she calls that orthopedist, but can't get an appointment until Thursday. Thursday? God. "Is this an emergency?" she's asked.

"Well, I guess not," she answers, thinking, This stinks. Should she take him to the hospital after school? Instead, he goes to ice hockey practice, without telling her.

"You are amazing," she says later. They argue, but not in real anger, about his leg and the possible consequences. He takes more painkillers. Puts himself back on the couch.

"Mom, you just don't understand," he says adamantly. "I have to do this."

By Tuesday evening, the two of them have become good at icing, wrapping, and medicating this mess of an emergency. He actually plays in a game but not well. Exhaustion and pain win over his will.

On Wednesday, her husband arrives home early, having caught an all-night, red-eye flight from California. A car service drops him off before 6 A.M., and she is so relieved. They tiptoe into their son's room and turn on the bedside reading light.

"Let me look at this leg," he whispers.

"Dad, it really hurts."

"Okay. I know. We're gonna take care of it right away."

Two hours later in the emergency room at Middleton, she puts her head between her knees to keep from fainting—a trick her mother taught her.

The leg is broken but not obviously. She's thankful for this crumb. If it had been more obvious, she certainly wouldn't have let him walk around, play ice hockey, and muscle his way around her best mothering instincts. Right? Oh, maybe. The ligaments running on either side of the back of his knee were so strong that they actually yanked a small bone, breaking it. Not easy to detect but definitely dangerous, the ER doctor explains to them. If he had gone for another day or two, he might have done real long-term damage. In fact, when the leg, which he has been dragging and painfully stiffening at a crooked angle for more than ninety-six hours, is straightened and popped into position, her son passes out. She was okay then and holding his hand as he was revived by the nurse.

"I am so sorry that I let this go," she says, crying. "Stupid. Stupid. Stupid. Why didn't I take you straight to the emergency room on Saturday night?" Her husband pats her back, affectionately.

In a cold sweat, her son mumbles, "Aw Mom, because I wouldn't let you." Then he grins. "I was pretty stubborn, huh?" The orthopedist is casting his leg with wet strips of fiberglass composite. She's never seen this done before and dries her eyes.

"Pretty crazy, huh?" he says.

"I guess."

"Both of us." He laughs. "Not as crazy as that stinky coach, though."

"For sure. Do you realize that you've been playing ice hockey on a broken leg?"

"Hey now, this is the kind of a break even experts can miss," her husband says. "I just looked at it on the X ray in the hallway. Don't beat yourselves up so badly."

By the next day at school, word of his broken leg has already spread. She drops him off in the circular front driveway. As he reaches into the backseat to retrieve his crutches, a crowd gathers on the sidewalk to get the details. She hears someone say, "Hey, way to go. I hear you've been playing ice hockey on a broken leg?"

Leaning back into the open passenger window and smiling across to her, he says, "Thanks, Mom." As she drives away, she thinks, maybe, just maybe, this is how high school winners and legends are born. At least epithets like *wimp* may get banished from the bench.

"Do you realize that crazy coach started borrowing my son's skates?" she says. "I'm not kidding. Who knows why he would want to do that, but my son saw it as no big deal and thought it was actually kind of cool. I couldn't believe the gall of that man." Meanwhile, throughout February and then into March, her son never missed a practice or a game, and got back into his own skates on the ice for the ceremonies at the division championship in early April. Later, teammates voted him co-captain for the next season. She was so proud.

"Want to hear something truly weird?" she asks me.

"What?"

"That creep, the coach—and you know, he didn't return for the next season—wouldn't wear socks inside those three-hundred-dollar skates. There he was, barefoot, in my son's skates." If you ask me, the truth is . . . he was the real loser.

The Art of Imperfection

U nless we are pressed up against an emotional wall or caught crying about something our boy has done or said, we tend to keep quiet about those deep, dark concerns for our sons' sanity and safety. I have a friend who retreated from all social encounters after her oldest descended into a period of drug addiction. But did she need to withdraw? I don't think so. She sent herself into mourning and hasn't emerged even now that he seems to be recovering and living drug free and independently in New England.

Beating ourselves up as parents is easy. Why can't our lives look like the ones in the Hallmark family holiday commercials? Well, they don't. None of that is absolutely true and even the happiest occasions, when life might look perfect, are often tinged with what's next, what if, and a sad song playing beneath the surface. As author Marianne Williamson says in *A Woman's Worth*, "Forget looking for earthly role models because there aren't many and even when we find them, they live their own lives and not ours." Give up the idea of perfection and you may soon see how imperfectly fun big boys can be. Cross your fingers. Keep talking and he will give you good stories even when he is being bad.

Perfectly Safe Is Impossible

She decides to send her third son to a boarding school in Rhode Island because he is doing so poorly at the local high school. This is tenth grade, and the counselor feels that he ought to have a more structured environment in order to succeed academically. He needs to pull his act together or the college acceptance game will come to a disastrous end. She expects a lot from her boys; the other two have been much more accommodating. Put this child in a safe place with fewer distractions and more rules, she is told. Some kids, especially boys, require lots of structure. Though not quite at military-level discipline, his new school will keep him in line.

He's a good kid and shares a lot of his life with her. Perhaps that's why he frightens her at times. Six weeks into his first semester away, he calls her at their regular Sunday evening time and says he's beat.

"Why are you so tired?" she asks. "What did you do this weekend?"

"Great party last night, Mom."

Oh no. Oh no. Heart thumps here. "On campus?" she asks.

"Nah."

"Did your RA know you were gone?"

"Of course, we signed ourselves out for the night."

"You can do that?"

"Mom, we're not in prison here," he answers, showing a little frustration now.

One of his roommates knew someone, who knew someone else, who had been e-mailed about a bash near their campus. So, the two ended up hiking the distance, having a wild time, and, somewhere around daybreak, he and this new best friend found themselves sleeping in a sand trap on the local golf course.

"We woke up to golf balls flying overhead," he says. "Crazy, huh?"

"Right," she answers, her mind racing back to all that official education-ese on controlled, safe environments away from the distractions of ordinary public high school social life.

"Why would guys get up so early just to play golf?" he wonders. "They must be crazy."

"You think they're crazy?" she says, allowing a little sarcasm to get loose here. She doesn't dare say, Thanks for sharing all this with me. He may stop sharing, and that would be even worse.

"Are you okay?"

"Sure."

And so is she. At least she didn't have to pick him up at the golf course at 6 A.M. She could sleep in on her own private Sunday morning. That much is true, even if the tightly controlled, safely structured environment her experts advertised is far from foolproof. The truth is, there just is no place on the parenting map called perfection. He's in a perfect place for the time being because she isn't spending all of her time thinking and worrying about him. The distance has let both of them grow independently, and their phone conversations have become anticipated events, not the dreaded showdowns they had been at home. This boy, she knows, had to fly away from home in order to appreciate her. A school offering cool discipline is a good idea, even when he's demonstrated that he can get around the rules.

"Promise me you won't party off campus again?" she asks, sounding almost casual, whereas in the past she would have been furious.

"Aw, Mom, I promise. That was kind of crazy, I guess."

The Ultimate Art of Unconditional Love

You're tired and under stress about (1) money? (2) mate? (3) work? (4) health? (5) home? (6) kids? (7) one or maybe two teenage boys?

Pick one, or more, for yourself, and keep in mind what the director of New York University Hospital's Stress Disorders Services once said to me: "Chronic stress is like having one foot on the accelerator of a car with the other foot on the brake. We wind up stripping our gears."

Now, with that thought held firmly in place, consider the fact that teenage boys aren't always easy to like. You can admit it here. No one else is listening. Yes, of course, we love them, but when the phone rings and it's been a car accident, an arrest, a disaster at school, a fight outside a club where he was forbidden to go . . . emotions run straight toward deep disappointment and outright fear. Will he survive? (Seriously, kids get killed and we all know it.) Can you hang in there? You can't give up. You just can't.

When was the last time you took a nap, read a novel, had fun with a friend, went shopping for new underwear (alone) or in search of what you used to love about parenting? Do it—so you can find something to laugh about with your son. Give yourself a break to restore your ability to love unconditionally. Feed yourself first, and don't apologize for being needy. You are not in an endurance contest here with this kid, although it may feel like that when his hostility and adolescent gambits block and rock our best intentions. Finding something to enjoy about this stage of parenting may test all your creative powers, but your enjoyment is the key to his future.

Wal-Mart after Christmas is a crazy place. In northern New Jersey, I'm in line at the checkout and can't help watching a dark-haired, harried mother of five boys who appear to range from fourteen down to twin toddlers in two carts. (Yes, I counted. Big families like this one are rare nowadays.) One of the twins obviously has a cold, because the area of skin around his nose is nasty red and mucus clogs the nostrils. At least three of the boys are begging for something she isn't buying today. They are a ragtag crew, intent on what looks like torture. I say all this not to be mean but to let you know how unlovable these boys were at this moment in her life.

It's nearly noon. She glances at me, runs her hand through her hair, and says, "I haven't even combed my hair today."

I smile. "You look fine."

She's interrupted from this brief adult exchange

by another urgent request for candy, or was it a toy? "No, we aren't buying anything else," she says to a middle-sized boy. In one of her carts is a new vacuum cleaner.

"I ran out to the grocery store to buy milk and when I came back, my vacuum was on fire. They blew it up," she tells me. A big boy behind her, already taller than his petite mom, chimes in. "Yeah, it's still smoking in our yard."

She turns back to me and is now laughing. "Can you imagine? They blew up the vacuum." All five boys, even the most recent whiner in the other cart, are now looking at me, amazed at how their mother tells the story with that optimistic twist to color their morning of adventure. What could have been an angry disaster or punishable act of mischief is turning into a happy memory. Aha.

"Aren't they amazing?" she says to me. "I could kill them." But of course, she loves them too much. They know it. She knows it.

■ ■

Dig Deep and Think of Yourself as an Artist of Human Nature

So, tell your own story. Right here. No gimmicks.

Has he been in trouble with drugs or alcohol?
Is he failing in school?
Has he totaled your car?
Did you find empty cases of beer in your backyard?

Do you fear what his taste in friends is saying about him?

Has he lied about his whereabouts?

Is he fighting with his father?

What about his clothes, social life, taste in music, mood swings, displays of anger?

Do his piercings and tattoos make you nervous?

Is he withdrawn?

Have you questioned flashes of rage?

Does he act as if he despises you?

Have you cried yourself to sleep?

Choose a topic and story near and dear to you and your teenager. Be honest about body image, puberty, sex, girls, alcohol, drugs, peer pressure, school, sports, failures, car accidents, friendships, depression, anger, divorce, brothers, sisters, violence, race, religion, prejudice. . . . Tell the truth and make yourself the heroine you are.

What's the craziest thing he's ever done? What's the craziest reaction you've ever had?

What are your biggest fears? What are his? Have you asked him about them?

What do you fight about?

What do you laugh about?

What makes you proud of him?

Would he turn to you for advice?

What are your secrets for staying sane?

Who is he? Who are you?

Aw Mom . . .

Fill in your *Oh Boy!* blanks.

_____

_____

_____

ABOUT THE AUTHOR

MARYANN BUCKNUM BRINLEY has been writing about children, families, heroines, and health for decades from her home office in Upper Montclair, New Jersey. She is also a publications editor and writer at the University of Medicine and Dentistry of New Jersey, and she has recently been concentrating on rum because of a family Caribbean venture, the Saint Kitts Rum Company, makers of award-winning Brinley Gold flavored rums.